J. Malcolm Finlaw

P9-AOY-322

Presented by Newburgh Y.P.U.

Jan 26, 1951

I KEPT MY POWDER DRY

JOHN COBURN

I Kept My Powder Dry

By

REV. JOHN COBURN, D.D.

THE RYERSON PRESS ~ TORONTO

To the Memory of

JAMES AND ANNIE ELIZABETH COBURN, *my parents,*

and

JOHN BARTHOLOMEW CAMPBELL, *a village schoolmaster,*

AND TO

SUSANNA WESLEY COBURN, *my wife,*

This Book is Gratefully Dedicated by the Author.

INTRODUCTION

This book is not an autobiography, although circumstances made unavoidable the frequent use of the first person singular. For twenty-five years I was a Methodist pastor in Ontario on Mission Fields, rural circuits, in village, town and city churches, down in the slums and up "on the hill." Then for another twenty-five years I served the Church as a Secretary of Evangelism and Social Service with a parish that included all of Canada, Newfoundland and Bermuda. This gave me a great variety of experience and enabled me to meet a host of interesting people.

These stories have been told by the fireside to friends all over Canada. Many of these have insisted that I ought to put them in printed form. It has been urged upon me as a duty to Canada because they depict types of people and social conditions that are rapidly disappearing.

The stories have been written in odd moments snatched from a rather busy life—some of them on railroad trains, steamboats and in hotel bedrooms. As it is my first offence in writing a book I hope I shall be forgiven. The voice not the pen has been my chief instrument of expression. I hope therefore that my readers will be tolerant towards defects in the work which some of them will doubtless discover, and that these defects will not lessen their pleasure in meeting some of the splendid and interesting people to whom I introduce them. Most of those of whom I have written have passed on. In some cases to avoid embarrassment to relatives and friends I have used fictitious names. Apart from that I have taken but few liberties with the facts.

My wife, who has been by my side for over fifty years, and who has personal knowledge of nearly all the characters and incidents herein referred to, has helped me greatly by stimulating and at times correcting my recollections by her own.

I am under deep obligation to Miss Pearl McCarthy and my daughter Miss Kathleen Coburn of Victoria College for sympathetic and critical reading of the manuscript and for many helpful suggestions.

JOHN COBURN.

Toronto,
September 1950.

CONTENTS

PAGE

PROLOGUE xi

1. A BOY PREACHER'S EXPERIENCES 1

2. THE FENIANS ARE COMING 15

3. ALGOMA LIFE 22

4. A PIONEER CASE IN CHILD WELFARE WORK . . 33

5. A COUNTRY PARSON 45

6. THE CHURCH AT TERRA NOVA 60

7. BOUTS WITH JOHN BARLEYCORN . . . 68

8. MORE BOUTS WITH JOHN BARLEYCORN . . 80

9. HERE COMES THE BRIDE 92

10. THE RUNAWAYS 101

11. THE FIGHT FOR A CLEAN STAGE . . . 112

12. SOCIAL WORK 128

13. AN EPISODE IN THE CHURCH UNION CONTROVERSY 137

14. HEROES OF FAITH AND ACTION . . . 144

15. SAINTS WITH LIMITATIONS 156

EPILOGUE 179

PROLOGUE

My Father and I

MY FATHER was born in Belfast, Ireland, in 1845. When a child of less than two years of age he lost his sight. Because of this handicap, he had so cultivated his senses of touch and hearing that they became unusually keen. He was educated in the Ulster Institution, a residential school in Belfast for the blind, deaf and dumb. In that school the Bible was a very prominent subject on the curriculum. Few people had as thorough a knowledge of the English Bible as he. It was a difficult thing for anyone to quote incorrectly any passage of the Scripture, in his hearing, without his detection. Often he would remark:

"If that chap had read that with his fingers, instead of his eyes, he would have remembered it better."

Father was born of a Church of Ireland family, attended the Sunday School, learned the Catechism and became familiar with the Anglican prayer book. In 1859 a great religious revival swept over the north of Ireland. The Presbyterian and Methodist churches gave leadership. Great meetings were held all over Ulster. It was said that, in Belfast and other towns, if anyone took his stand at a street corner and began to sing or speak a crowd would quickly assemble.

Father, a boy of fourteen at home on vacation, was caught in the mighty current. Attracted by Methodist theology which proclaimed the free Grace of God to all men, and also by the warmth and enthusiasm of the Methodist meetings, he at once joined the Wesleyan Church.

Before long it was discovered that the blind lad had an unusual gift of speech. The Methodist Class Meeting in which all converts were expected to tell of their experiences in the Christian life, was a means of discovering and developing such talent. There is no doubt, that the old Class Meeting was a major force in the development of Methodism. It produced a great host of lay preachers, who carried Methodism and established Methodist societies in many communities unreached by ordained ministers.

In 1913 I visited Belfast. I was asked to preach in one of the large Mission Halls at a Sunday evening service. There I met Thomas McCord, a little old man of whom I had often heard father speak, and who, in his young manhood was his most intimate friend. Next day he took me round those parts of Belfast frequented by father. We visited the Ulster Institution where the principal showed me the desk at which father sat when a scholar there. As we walked the streets Mr. McCord stopped several times and said:

"Now John, right on this corner your father often preached and usually I was with him."

He also informed me that the Mission Hall in which I had preached was built on the site of the little Wesleyan Chapel in which father had preached his trial sermon to be made a local preacher.

"And John, the Reverend Wesley Garde, one of Ireland's foremost Methodist preachers, was the minister appointed to sit in judgment on your father's sermon, and he is still alive and lives here in Belfast."

That evening a telephone call to Mr. Garde's house revealed that he was at the Methodist College. As I was leaving for Liverpool that night I lost no time. Mr. Garde though a very old man, was presiding at a meeting of the

College Board. Word was sent in to him that a Methodist minister from Canada wished to see him. A secretary came out and said that I was to go with him into the meeting. To my surprise and a little embarrassment, I found the whole Board standing on their feet to welcome the visitor from across the seas.

I told Mr. Garde who I was and asked him if he remembered the young blind boy upon whose sermon he had sat in judgment many years ago.

"Indeed I do," said he. "He was a fine lad. I had no hesitation in recommending him. And now you tell me that you, his son, are the minister of a Methodist church in the great city of Toronto? I tell you sir, we are proud and grateful. Irish Methodism rejoices in her sons all over the world. We recognize you as one of them. Thank you a thousand times for coming to see me. May God bless you in your work and please convey my heartiest good wishes to your honoured father."

Father had a very high ideal of the work of preaching the Gospel. He was strongly convinced that no man had a right to undertake the work unless he was definitely called of God. He also believed that one so called could refuse only at his peril. While he felt he was called to preach he steadfastly refused to be ordained. He did not think that one with such a handicap as blindness could fulfil all the duties of a minister. All through his active life he was a free-lance, preaching, lecturing, conducting evangelistic services and campaigning for temperance and other good causes.

He came to Canada in 1871. There were only four people in the Dominion that he knew, two cousins and their wives. He thought one family lived in Toronto and the other in Hamilton, but he was not sure. Within a few hours of arrival in Toronto he had located one of his cousins. He soon made many friends. He made himself known to the Methodist people and in a short time was busy at his beloved work of preaching.

He had a strong voice and was much in demand for the camp meetings which featured Methodist work in those days. Speaking in the open air is usually hard on the voice but it did not seem to affect him at all. At one of the camp meetings held near Owen Sound he was persuaded to act as assistant to a minister who had a huge circuit of ten appointments.

One round of three churches had such bad roads that no buggy could be taken. The preacher had to go either on foot or on horseback. They secured for father a quiet little pony that had been trained to follow another horse. So a man on horseback led the way, Father and his pony followed. The round trip was thirty-five miles. Father had never had his foot in a stirrup before, but he made the trip and conducted three services on the way. He did this not once, but several times.

While on this circuit he met my mother. I have been told that she was one of the prettiest girls in the community. A preacher friend said one day to father:

"Brother Coburn, how comes it that a man who cannot see comes along and picks out such a pretty girl for a wife, and right from under the noses of a lot of fine fellows too?"

"Oh well you know, there is more than one way of seeing," was the reply.

His choice was truly a wise one. When I think of what my mother did for him and for us, their children, I am filled with wonder.

Father was a loyal Britisher, an ardent Protestant, a devoted Methodist, and an uncompromising foe of the liquor traffic. During a fiercely contested temperance campaign in Huron County, where we lived for several years, it came to his ears that the "wets" had dubbed him "The Blind Devil." He was very proud of that. Next to the love and confidence of his friends, he gloried in the opposition of certain of his enemies. He was a man of the utmost courage. To run away from a duty because it might be

JAMES COBURN

The Author's Father

"No, I'm not a blind preacher (I trust)
but a preacher who happens to be blind."

dangerous, or to fail to perform a task because it might be a bit unpleasant, was, in his eyes, one of the greatest of sins. His mind was always alert, and he seldom failed to give an appropriate answer when called for.

While serving as junior pastor on the Artemesia circuit, he attended a tea meeting on one occasion. There was a man in the neighbourhood by the name of Flesher, who was rather prominent in the little village, but had the reputation of being a bit of a philanderer. As his wife was a fine woman, highly esteemed by all, Mr. Flesher was none too popular, especially with the church people. At this tea meeting, Mr. Flesher joined the group of which father was one. He apparently made up his mind to take a bit of a rise out of the young preacher. It will be remembered that in those days the Methodist rules were very strict in regard to "worldly" amusements. Dancing was one of the things forbidden. So Mr. Flesher, after being introduced to father said:

"I suppose Mr. Coburn like all other Methodists you are opposed to dancing."

"Well Mr. Flesher," father answered, "you understand of course, that owing to circumstances dancing can never be a personal issue with me, but it is one of the rules of our church. I believe in the rule and am ready to defend it."

"Then," said the other, "you claim to be wiser than Solomon."

"How do you make that out?"

"Now, Mr. Coburn, I understand you are well versed in the Scriptures. You surely know that Solomon said 'there is a time to dance.' So you are wiser than Solomon."

"Yes," said father, "I am afraid I must claim that in one particular I am wiser than Solomon."

"Oh indeed, that's interesting, I am sure we would all like to know in what particular you are wiser than Solomon," sarcastically replied Mr. Flesher. Father then said:

"Mr. Flesher, if God is ever good enough to give me the love of a true woman and I make her my wife, I will be completely satisfied, and will not find it necessary to be running after other women. In this I think I can fairly claim to be wiser than Solomon." The poor victim had nothing to say.

For years after their marriage, mother did father's reading for him. Later with the home and the children to care for she hadn't the time. When I had learned to read well enough, the duty became mine. My father and I were always great pals, often taking long walks together. He freely discussed with me the things we read. Theology, history and current events, especially politics, were the chief subjects. This experience was of very great value to me. In my early teens I had a good working knowledge of both Methodist discipline and doctrine. When I began to preach (before I was eighteen years old) I had a start that few students for the ministry would have had.

Father had a wonderful memory. Often when I read to him he would stop me and ask that I read a paragraph again. Then he would repeat it, and almost word for word. He would use that as a quotation in a sermon or lecture.

His sense of hearing was very acute. It was almost impossible to do anything in the house unknown to him. On one occasion he was down in the city at a meeting. We lived on the outskirts. At mother's suggestion I went to meet him. We had board sidewalks in those days. I saw him coming along a quiet street. No one else was in sight. By quietly touching his cane to the inside of the sidewalk once in a while, he kept on a perfectly straight line. He disliked very much to hear a blind man tapping continually with his cane, "advertising his affliction" he called it.

I thought I would test him, so I walked steadily toward him without speaking. When within about ten paces I saw him turn his head slightly to one side as if listening for something. I marched on past him without stopping. I had

not taken more than three or four steps past him when he
stopped and turned around:

"I say, John, is that you?"

Father knew and loved Toronto. Up until 1920 he
travelled freely all over the city alone by night or day.
Until near the end he did not have to contend with automobiles. The bicycles gave him the most difficulty.

"The pesky things, you can't hear them," he would say.

One day in downtown Toronto as he went to cross a
street, his cane caught in the wheel of a passing bicycle
and was broken, a part of it still remained in his hand. He
made his way to the nearby office of a friend, who took
him to a store where a new cane was bought. I doubt if
any of the family would ever have known of this, but for
the fact that the new cane had to be accounted for. We
learned at times of minor accidents which were never
reported. He also travelled all over Ontario by rail. Indeed
he was quite an authority on railroad trains and connections.

Father had a wonderful faculty for making friends. On
this account and no doubt because of his affliction, people
usually were very kind to him. Sometimes they were a little
too kind. One thing he resented was being babied. He
didn't want anyone to do anything for him that he could
do for himself, though he understood the offers were kindly
meant, and was gracious if firm in the occasional refusal.
He insisted on taking care of his own clothes and shining his
shoes. When his things were washed, mother put them in a
certain place. When he wanted a collar or a pair of socks
he went and got them. When he started out on a preaching
or lecturing tour he packed his own grip. When he began
preaching, Methodist preachers wore long narrow white
ties, tied in a bow. The first Sunday he wore one of these,
a lady tied it for him. He made up his mind "never again."
So when he retired that night he sat down on his bed and
untied the thing. Then he worked away tying and untying,
until he had mastered the problem. No one ever tied a

bow for him after that, and no one could tie a bow more neatly than he.

One night father was being entertained at the home of a friend. As he had never been in the house before, his host took him up to his room, and led him around showing him the location of each article of furniture, including the mirror.

"Now Brother Coburn, when you are in bed, just call and I will come and put out the light for you."

Father burst out laughing. "What's the joke?" asked the friend.

"Joke? Why man, what earthly good would a lamp do me?"

"Oh," said the other much embarrassed, "I'm sorry, I forgot, but it does seem awfully queer to come away and leave a man in the dark."

"Never mind that, one thing I can guarantee, I can get around a dark room a lot better than you can."

I am stating only the general opinion of those who heard him when I say that James Coburn was a forceful and effective preacher. He had, as stated, a thorough knowledge of the scriptures. For one whose access to literature was necessarily limited, he had a wide vocabulary and singularly good command of language.

Strange to say, one of his most inspiring sermons and one he loved to preach was from the text—"And the Light shineth in the darkness." No doubt the fact that he himself was a living demonstration of the truth of the text, increased the effectiveness of the sermon.

He had also a soul-shaking sermon on the Last Judgment, from the text "Behold He cometh with clouds, and every eye shall see Him, and they also that pierced Him, and all the nations of the earth shall wail because of Him. Even so, Amen." It was the only sermon in which he was ever known to refer directly or indirectly to his affliction. In this sermon, after depicting in graphic terms the glory and the terror of the Great Assize, he would comment on the phrase, "every eye shall see Him." He always offered a brief apology for making a personal reference and then with an elation of spirit that never failed to move a congregation deeply:

"Yes friends, every eye shall see Him, even these eyes of mine that have never consciously looked in the face of mother or wife or child, shall see Him. The first sight to fall upon their enraptured vision will be that of the King in His beauty! The King upon the throne."

Psychologists tell us that often something that happens in early childhood may affect one's whole life. One day when I was a small boy playing in our house with my sisters, a friend came in, he suggested that father would be making a preacher of me.

"No indeed, I'll do nothing of the kind. If I tried that I'd be sure to make a botch of it, and you know I'd rather John would be a good tinker, than a botch of a preacher. If God calls him to be a preacher, I'll be very happy."

"Oh well," said the man, "if he's half as good as his father he'll do."

"And if he's not a lot better than his father, it'll be a shame on him."

Father's casual remark shocked me greatly. I was firmly convinced that my father was the greatest and best man in all the world. With all the ardour of a little boy's heart I worshipped him. To know that father expected me to be better than he was just overwhelming. Of course, in later years I came to understand what he meant, that with sight, many opportunities would be mine that were denied him. But the memory of that hour never left me. In more than fifty years of ministry I have often been tempted, like other men, to avoid unpleasant situations and disagreeable duties, but always that face with its sightless eyes would rise up before me and that voice would ring in my ears.

1

A BOY PREACHER'S EXPERIENCES

1. *First Converts*

THE Mono Road circuit in the Methodist Church, consisting of eight small rural churches, was situated about thirty miles from Toronto. It had been manned by three preachers—an ordained Minister and two probationers. The Conference of 1892 was able to send only one probationer. Rev. John Mahan, a genial Irishman, a good friend of my father was appointed as the Minister. In August he invited me to spend a Sunday on his field. When I arrived he said to me:

"John, how would you like to come up here and preach every Sunday during the conference year? This young man they have sent me and I can handle the pastoral work, but we are a man short on Sundays. You could do your college work during the week and come up here on Saturday night. When railway fares and other expenses are paid, there won't be much money in it for you, but there will be a little, and it will help with your college expenses. Then, the experience in preaching will be good for you, and when you come up as a candidate before Conference next June, the fact that you have been preaching steadily for nearly

1

a year will give you a fine standing. What do you say, my boy?"

Here was something I hadn't counted on. I was only eighteen years old. True, I had preached a few times at various places in and near Toronto, but this meant undertaking to preach every Sunday. With much labour I had managed to produce half a dozen or more sermons. Could I manage to produce enough to keep me going for nearly a whole year? Mr. Mahan seemed to sense my difficulty. "Don't be afraid, John," he said very kindly. "You couldn't start preaching in an easier place. You see, it takes three weeks to make the complete circuit of all the appointments, so the number of sermons you will have to get up will be small. It isn't as if you had to face the same congregation once or twice each Sunday."

I had fully made up my mind to be a Minister. I would have greatly liked to be a lawyer, but I was convinced God had called me to this work. In spite of my youth and lack of experience, I was thrilled with the prospect of getting at the job. So under the kind assurance and persuasion of my Irish friend, I agreed.

For the balance of the Conference Year I preached every Sunday on the Mono Road circuit. As I had no horse, it was arranged that until permanent arrangements could be made, one of the church members would meet me at the train on Saturday night, take me to his home for the weekend, drive me to my appointments on Sunday and then take me back to the railway station on Monday morning. On each of two Sundays I conducted three services; on the third, I had only two.

Very early in the year, I was entertained at the home of Mr. John Dixon, a farmer of Sand Hill. On Sunday night I preached in the Sand Hill Church.

That little church was like hundreds of others in the Province of Ontario. It was built by the pioneers, largely with their own hands and without the aid of an architect.

The church was about thirty-six feet long and twenty-six feet wide and would comfortably accommodate a congregation of one hundred. At the rear of the church was a shed providing the necessary shelter for the horses that had brought most of the congregation to the church. The church was plain and simple, heated by wood stoves and lit by coal-oil lamps set at various places in the church.

The congregation was composed almost entirely of farmers and their families. They were sincere, God-fearing people who took their religion seriously. Barring unfavourable weather conditions, the preacher could always count on a full house at Sand Hill. A group of young people, farmers' sons and daughters formed the choir, and were accompanied by a small reed organ. While it is not likely that their music would win a prize at a modern music festival, it came from the heart and, unlike some church music of today, was a real part of the service of worship.

The church was not only the religious, but also the social centre of the community. There were no moving pictures, no telephones, no motor cars. It was the usual custom for a young man to hitch up the best horse the farm afforded, carefully groomed, and in a well-washed buggy drive his girl to the church service and take her home again at the conclusion. And if some of those young folk did a little hand holding surreptitiously in the service, who could blame them? Sand Hill Church was a much better place in which to find a wife than a public dance hall or a beverage room. The church service was practically the only regular opportunity the people of the community had to get together. So, after the Benediction had been pronounced, one would see little groups of men here and of women there, discussing matters of local interest—the health of the people, any cases of sickness or death, a letter from a boy or girl that had gone to the city to school or to get a job. These and other similar matters were subjects of conversation.

Gossip you say, yes, perhaps, but kindly and friendly gossip prompted by the interest they had in one another.

On the evening of my first service in that church it was crowded to the door. For an eighteen-year-old lad to stand up and face such a group was not an easy task. Here were veterans in the Christian life, some of whom were old enough to be my grandfather or my grandmother, at least two were experienced lay preachers. But as I looked down into their upturned faces, I saw sincerity, earnestness and sympathy for the boy preacher. Then in harmony with the prevailing Methodist custom during the progress of the sermon a few reverent and earnest "Amens" or "Praise the Lords" were interjected. These things gave me courage. I preached from the text "Behold I stand at the door and knock." It was a simple, boyish appeal to all to open their hearts to Christ. I was about to announce the last hymn and close the service, when it occurred to me that there might be someone in the congregation who was just ready to respond to the appeal I had made, and that if I sent them away without securing definite commitment, the good impression might wear off and so the opportunity of winning a convert be lost.

So on the spur of the moment I said: "I wonder if there is anyone here who is ready to open the door of his life and let the Master come in, or in other words begin the Christian life. If there is such a one will you please indicate it by raising your hand?"

Without a moment's hesitation a young lad about my own age lifted his hand. I then did what was the Methodist usage in such cases, I stepped down in front of the pulpit, announced a hymn and invited this young man and any others who felt as he did to come and kneel at the altar.

"When we finish singing this hymn we will all bow in prayer and two or three of the brethren will lead us."

It was my first service in that church. The people were all strangers to me but I was quite sure that in a group of that size in a Methodist Church there would be those who could be depended on to do as I asked. I was not disappointed. The prayer meeting did not last long, but at its conclusion, Willie Dixon rose from the altar with a radiant face. Willie was the nephew of my host and lived with his uncle as one of the family. When we all returned from the service there was great rejoicing in the Dixon home.

I walked on air for days. In the Methodist Discipline there was a series of questions to be asked of all who claimed to be called of God to preach. These questions were originally compiled by John Wesley and had been handed down as part of the Methodist tradition. One of these questions was: "Has he any fruit?" I had declared before the official board of my church that I believed I was called of God to preach. On that assurance they had licensed me. Now here was some fruit. But there was more to follow.

Mr. Dixon's own son, also called William and about the same age as his cousin, was attending high school in Brampton, eleven or twelve miles away. This boy, a good lad in every way, had not taken the decisive step and given himself definitely to Christ. His father and mother were anxious that he should do so. Without my knowledge, Mr. Dixon went to Mr. Mahan and asked that on my next visit to Sand Hill, three weeks hence, I would again be their guest. That being arranged, they had their son Willie come home for the week-end. Then on Sunday morning Willie's father asked him to drive me to my appointments. He very willingly agreed. Before we left the house for my first service Mr. Dixon took me aside and said:

"Mr. Coburn, we asked to have you with us today and brought Willie home, hoping that what happened to his cousin three weeks ago will happen to him. He is a good boy, all he needs is just to accept Christ. Now Mr. Coburn, while you and Willie are away, Mother and I will pray that God may help you to lead our boy to Christ this day."

Some responsibility to lay upon a boy of eighteen! At the close of the afternoon service Willie and I got into the buggy to drive to his father's home for supper. Willie said to me: "Mr. Coburn I tell you, I never felt as much like being a Christian in my life as I did in that service."

"You don't know how glad I am to hear you say that," I replied.

"If an invitation had been given would you have gone forward?"

"I certainly would."

"Well then, Willie you'll get an invitation tonight in your own home church. After all that'll be a better place for you to take your stand, among your own people, your neighbours and friends."

"Yes," he answered, "I guess that's right. I'll do it anyway."

When we arrived at his home, I took his father aside and told him what had happened.

"Thank God," he said very reverently, "how happy his mother will be."

After supper, it came on a heavy rainstorm which continued until the hour of service and after. Some of the family said there was no use in going to church, that there wouldn't be anybody there. But Willie, his father and I knew something of which the others were ignorant. We had business to do in Sand Hill Church that night, and mighty important business too. So the three of us piled into a buggy intended for two and went to the church through the rain. There were about a dozen people in the congregation. I preached a very short sermon and then announced that there was one of our number who wished to make a public confession of Christ as his Saviour and Lord. Willie came forward and, as he said, found a peace he had never known before. He finished his work at High School and went to Victoria College where he decided that he too was called to the ministry. He volunteered for mission work in

Saskatchewan. There for many years he served the church with great faithfulness and success.

He was there during the period of the great tide of immigration that came to Canada. He helped push back the frontiers of the Church, and to lay the foundation of the Church's work in many communities in Saskatchewan. He met sudden death in a motor accident. When his body was brought back to Ontario for burial, I was asked to take part in the funeral service. I told the story of his conversion much as I have told it here. After the service was over, a middle aged man came forward and shaking me warmly by the hand said:

"Don't you know me?"

"I can't say I do but there is something about you that is familiar," I replied.

"Well there ought to be," he said with a smile. "I am the other Willie Dixon. I want to tell you Mr. Coburn that although it is forty years ago and during those forty years I have not been as good a Christian as I ought to have been, I never got away from what happened that Sunday night in Sand Hill Church. I am still on the Way and my determination is by the Grace of God to continue to the end."

2. In Irish Mulmur

In June, 1893, I was appointed junior preacher on the Mulmur Circuit in the County of Dufferin. The circuit consisted of six small rural churches and was served by an ordained minister and a probationer. Each of us preached three times each Sunday. In that way each church had one service each Sunday and each preacher visited each place once in two weeks. The people were nearly all immigrants from the north of Ireland, or their descendants. They were warm hearted and hospitable. They were all ardent Protestants. From the days of the early settlement of the Township, it was understood that Roman Catholic settlers could easily find some more congenial place in which to live than Mulmur. Most of the men belonged to one of the Orange lodges of which there were several in the Township. They were a church-going, God-fearing people. Though they were intelligent, few had had many educational advantages. The older generation were pioneers. To cut down the trees, uproot the stumps, clear the land, which itself was rough and hilly, involved a struggle that taxed to the utmost both time and strength available. These pioneers saw to it that each community was supplied with a school and a church. So far as higher learning was concerned, there were neither the facilities nor the necessary cash. I cannot now remember any person in these six congregations who had a university education. Very few had been to high school. The second generation had received the training afforded by "the little red school house."

My predecessor had boarded with an estimable family in a comfortable farm house situated conveniently in the centre of the circuit, but this family, Rutledge by name, had sent word to Conference that they didn't care to board the "praicher" any longer. Rev. W. F. Ferrier, a most sincere, devoted man was the minister in charge. At Conference he spoke to me about this, saying that it was a great pity, as the Rutledge home was a very comfortable one and very conveniently situated and that he did not know where on the circuit I could find a suitable boarding place. I told my father about the difficulty. Being an Irishman he knew and understood these people of Mulmur well. "Och," he said, "yon man Ferrier is a good man, but what does a Scotchman like him know about handling these Ulster men in Mulmur? Now John, you do what I tell you and I don't think you will have much difficulty. The Rutledges are fine people. The old man comes from County Fermanagh from a little place called Lisbellau near Enniskillen. I have preached there and know it well." Then father told me a lot of things about that part of Ireland. "Now then," he said, "you drive up to Rutledge's and say: 'Well I have come.' Get hold of the old man and talk to him about Ireland and especially Fermanagh and Lisbellau. You'll not have to go any farther for a boarding house, or I am mistaken."

On a very hot July day, I drove my horse and buggy from Toronto to Rosemont where Mr. Ferrier lived. I told him I wanted to go to Rutledge's. He said he did not think it was any use but if I wanted to, he and his wife would go with me. We arrived just as the men were coming in from the fields for supper. Jim, one of the "boys" (a mere lad of forty-five) greeted me in the lane. I jumped out of my buggy and said: "Well I've come." He laughed and said: "So I see."

He took my horse and put it in the stable. I then espied the old man and made for him. The veteran Methodist, seventy-four years of age, gave the young preacher a really warm Irish welcome.

I said: "You are from Fermanagh, aren't you brother Rutledge?"

"Why yes, from Lisbellau," he answered.

"Yes, that's just over beyond Enniskillen."

"Aye, my boy, you're right, were you over there?"

"No sir, but my father has told me a lot about Fermanagh."

I went on to ask him more questions and to release some of the information with which my father had primed me. The old man grasped my arm and we walked to the house together.

"I know your father well. Many's the time I have heard him praich. Good sarmons too. The thrue Gospel and he is a rale Irishman at that. And say, you look a lot like him."

Before we arrived at the house, the old man and the preacher lad of nineteen had formed a friendship which was to last until the old man finished his course and passed on to a better world. Next followed introductions to the rest of the family: Mrs. Rutledge, of whose motherly care I was to be the subject; Sarah, the daughter, who had sacrificed herself and her prospects of a home of her own to care for her aged father and mother and who managed the house; Joe, the younger son, who ran the farm and who was to be my chum. Then we had supper, and what a supper and what stories and laughter! After this "The Book" was given to Mr. Ferrier. He read a chapter and asked me to pray. In those days among Methodists, fervent audible Amens were quite frequent both in public services and in family devotion. Old Mr. Rutledge was a real old Methodist and could be depended on to do his full duty along that line. After prayer, he said to me: "Why me boy, with me eyes shut, I could have swore it was your father himself that was doin' that prayin'. You are as like him as two peas."

At this point Mr. Ferrier put in: "Now what are you people going to do with this young man?"

Before anyone had time to speak, I managed to say: "Well I will tell you this, Mr. Ferrier, I am very tired. My horse that brought me from Toronto is tired. I am not going one foot farther this night. If these good people have a bed to spare, I'll be glad. If not, I can sleep on the floor or any place, but for tonight at any rate this is where I stay."

"Aye," said the old man, "indade and no one would ask you to go further, and ye won't have to sleep on the flure nayther. And say, Mother" (addressing his better half) "we did send word that we wouldn't keep the praicher any longer but can't we change that? Surely we can look after this young Irishman."

"Well," said the little old lady, who up to this time had taken small part in the conversation, "it all depends on Sarah. She has the work to do and she should have the say."

"Well Sarah, what do you say?" her father inquired.

"Maybe Mr. Coburn comin' from the city wouldn't be satisfied with the room we could give him."

"Where is it, show it to me, please." Sarah took me up the stairs and showed me a beautiful room, plenty large enough for bedroom and study combined. It had a door that opened to the east, out on a small verandah. There was spread before me one of the finest rural views to be found in Ontario. For thirty or forty miles there stretched the rolling hills of Mulmur, Tosorontio and other townships.

"May I have this room?" I said, addressing Sarah.

"Sure you can, if it suits you."

It did not take me long to get back downstairs and announce to all that Sarah and I had settled it and that for the coming year, this would be my home. Several months after this, one day at dinner, we had, as usual been passing jokes around. The old lady said:

"Aren't we the quare people? Didn't we make up our minds and send word to the Conference that we wouldn't board the young praicher any more and look here, he's with us as large as life."

"Och me," said the old man, "you know very well we couldn't turn a dasint young Irishman like this out on the road."

No boy away from his home for the first time ever received greater kindness than did the young preacher in question.

The first Sunday morning I put on old clothes and went out to the stable. Jim met me at the stable door, standing squarely in my way.

"Where are you goin'?"

"To the stable of course."

"What for?"

"Why to clean and harness my horse."

"Not today. Now you get away back to the house and get your proper Sunday clothes on. The horse will be at the door when you need him. This is no place for you on the Sabbath day."

Sure enough, Jim drove Charlie fully groomed to the door. I stepped into the buggy and drove off to my morning service. This ritual was followed every Sunday during my stay. Every Sunday night when I drove home after my day's work, the bedding and feed for my horse were in their place and all I had to do was to unharness the horse, put on its halter and tie it to the manger.

Mrs. Rutledge had very strong convictions about the keeping of the Sabbath. I had arrived at the Rutledge home on a Friday evening. Saturday I was very busy. I had to get settled in my new quarters and above all, make final preparations for preaching to three strange congregations on the morrow. Sunday morning after breakfast, I inquired for the shoe brush and blacking. The old lady looked at me very solemnly and said:

"Now, Mr. Coburn, though you are our praicher, you are only a boy and you are away from your mother for the first time, so I must tell you when you do wrong. Mr. Coburn, you should have polished your boots last night. The Sabbath is no day for such work, especially by a man going out to praich the Gospel to other people."

Every excuse was made for me by Sarah and her father. I was "strange to the place" and so was allowed to clean my boots before starting out on my journey, but it was made quite plain that this was not expected to occur again. For the sake of the dear old lady's peace of mind, I was always careful afterwards to polish my shoes on Saturday night.

My superintendent, Rev. W. F. Ferrier, was one of the best of men. Like many other early Methodist preachers, he had had very limited educational advantages but sought to make the very most of those he had. The Quarterly Meeting was a great event on a Methodist Circuit in those days. On one Sunday each quarter, the people assembled at one of the churches, the others being closed for the day.

After regular preaching service, they held what was called a love feast in which about an hour would be spent in personal testimonies by members of the church. This was followed by the communion service. The two preachers on the circuit took turns in preaching at this service. The people of the church at which the service was held always made preparations to entertain the visitors at dinner. It happened to be Mr. Ferrier's turn to preach at the February Quarterly Meeting. One day, a short time before, I found him reading Henry Drummond's book on *Natural Law in the Spiritual World.*

He said: "I'm going to preach on this theme at the Quarterly Meeting."

I was startled. I knew that Drummond's book dealt with issues which hardly came within the experience of the good folk of Mulmur.

"You will need to simplify it a good deal," I remarked.

"Oh yes, I know that. I will simplify it all right."

The Quarterly Meeting Sunday was a bright, cold winter's day. The church was packed. Mr. Ferrier placed at one side of the pulpit a rather pretty house plant and on the other a stone. He took for his text, "He that hath the Son, hath life and he that hath not the Son hath not life." The organic represented by the flower and the inorganic represented by the stone, were used as symbols of spiritual conditions. The good man had read and re-read Drummond's work so that he had become fairly steeped in not only the ideas but the very language of the book. Quite unintentionally he had memorized whole sections and in his sermon he recited page after page. As I sat up in the pulpit and looked down on the faces before me, I was very doubtful if half a dozen people in that congregation had any clear idea as to what it was all about. The "organic" and "inorganic" were referred to again and again. In fact they were the key words of the sermon. If you did not understand their meaning, the sermon would be meaningless. A goodly number of visitors had been at the Rutledge home for dinner that day. Mr. Rutledge and his family were too loyal to the church and preacher to offer any criticism or raise any questions in the presence of others, but after everybody had gone, the old man came to me and said: "I say John, what on earth did Ferrier mean this mornin' by this gaelic and higher gaelic he talked so much about?"

2

THE FENIANS ARE COMING

WHILE living in the Rutledge home, it was one of my delights to get the venerable George to tell me stories of the pioneer days. One of the most intensely interesting was that of the Fenian Raid scare. At that time Mr. Rutledge was a man in his prime, forty-seven years of age, strong and a hard worker. He and his good wife were busy clearing the land, making a home for themselves and their children.

The Fenian organization arose in Ireland and consisted of Roman Catholics who were exceedingly hostile to Britain and everything British. A branch of the organization was formed in the United States. At the close of the American Civil War in 1865 there were many Irish soldiers discharged from the Army. Many of these joined the Fenians. Armed bands were formed along the Canadian border from Detroit to the border of New Brunswick. The ambition of these fanatics was to attack and conquer Canada and annex it to the United States. The Government of the United States did nothing to suppress these bands. At that time there was considerable resentment towards Britain because of her attitude in the Civil War. There was also a lot of anti-British sentiment and threats of annexing Canada in some American newspapers. In May, 1866, a band of Fenians crossed over the Niagara River near Buffalo. There they were met by a body of Canadian volunteers. Nine Fenians were killed, many others wounded and the whole band put to flight. So ended one of the most hair-brained adventures ever attempted in the New World. In that day there were no telephones and few telegraph lines. Most of the Province was as yet untouched by railroads. Daily newspapers were practically unknown outside three or four cities and some towns. Under these circumstances the wildest rumours were broadcast. For many months the people of Ontario were kept in constant suspense, fearing the invasion from the South.

The strange story that follows was told me by Mr. Rutledge, who was one of the four hundred men who assembled at Rosemont on that occasion.

"You know," he said, "it was believed by us Mulmur people that it was all arranged that when the Fenians got this far, the Catholics of Ajala would rise and join them, march on Mulmur, murder us in our beds if they could and divide up our farms. In fact, it was believed that the Ajala people had it all planned as to who was to receive the different farms in Mulmar."

Ajala, it may be said, was the township whose northwest corner met Mulmur's south-east corner at the little village of Rosemont. It was composed largely of Irish Roman Catholics. Mr. Rutledge then proceeded to tell me that on a certain Sunday evening, a horseman, whose horse was covered with foam galloped along the south town line of Mulmur. He stopped at the first house on each concession and shouted:

"The Fenians have come and the Catholics of Ajala have riz. Warn all the men on your line and have every able-bodied man go to Rosemont as quickly as possible. Tell them to bring with them the best weapons they can find."

Rosemont was the meeting place of two other townships besides Mulmur and Ajala, namely Mono and Tosorontio.

These other two were like Mulmur, almost wholly Protestant. By midnight, four hundred men from these three townships met at Rosemont. They were armed with every kind of weapon, from the very latest and best muskets to pitchforks. Some who could find nothing better, just cut themselves a good stout club in the bush.

Here then were four hundred excited, angry Irishmen assembled for a fight. But where was the foe? No sign of him anywhere. What was to be done?

"Come on boys, let's march down to Ajala, and take the rebels on their own ground. No use waiting here!" So spoke Tom Gallaugher.

"Hear, hear," came from several sections of the crowd, others however counselled caution and delay. But the real hero of the occasion, the man whose courage and clear-headedness saved the day, was Dr. Robinson. He was the only doctor for miles around and was well known and respected by all—Protestant and Catholic. He mounted one of the sleighs and addressed the crowd.

"Men," said he, "you know I am right with you in defending our homes and our wives and children from any invader who may come. If any of such should appear I'll fight with the best of you as long as there is one man left to stand by my side. I think you good men of Mulmur, Mono and Tosorontio will give any such crowd a reception that they will never want repeated."

"Hurrah, hurrah," "Bully for the little doctor, he's got the right stuff in him."

"But men," he continued when the cheers had subsided, "we want to be very sure of what we are doing. I am strongly of the opinion that this is a false rumour. I have been down in Ajala today, visiting my patients and I saw not the slightest sign of any movement among the people. If a raid of this kind was being planned, surely there would have been some signs and you know I don't go around the country with my eyes shut. Now if we march down as is proposed, there will certainly be a fight with bloodshed. Probably some on both sides will be killed. If it comes out afterwards that these Ajala people were not planning to attack us, the whole country will blame us. It will be all our fault. Some of us would probably be tried for murder, and all of us will be liable to punishment for our action; so men, I beg of you be careful, be sure you're right before you act."

"Och Doctor—caution is all right but we all know what them fellows would do to us if they could. Now we're here and we're ready, let's go and give them a dose they won't forget." So spoke Jim Thompson.

He was supported by some of the young hotheads, and by some who had been imbibing freely in one of the taverns and whose belligerency had not been lessened by what they had drunk.

"Jim," said the doctor, "you're an Orangemen, aren't you?"

"Yes sorr, you bet I am, and a Royal Arch Purple Marksman at that."

"And a lot of the men here are Orangemen, aren't they?"

"Yes sorr, I guess most of them have rode the goat."

"Well didn't you and they (in the lodge) take a solemn oath of loyalty to the Queen, and to obey the laws of the land?"

"Yes sorr, of course we did."

"Now then, because of a wild rumour for which as yet there is no proof, you propose to disturb the Queen's peace and engage in an action that violates the law. What about your oath Jim?"

The doctor's words sobered Jim and the others too. Then one of the older men spoke up, "That sounds rale sensible doctor, but what can we do?" That was just what the doctor was waiting for.

"Well boys I have a plan that I think will work. I have a fresh team in the stable. I propose that you elect one of your number, anyone you like to go with me. We will drive down into the heart of Ajala and I promise you that on the first sign of any preparations to attack us, we will hurry back here and give you warning. You must remain here, and if an attack should be made we'll give the attackers a lesson they won't forget. If on the other hand this is a false alarm, we will not have made fools of ourselves and broken the law."

There was a lively discussion between the more belligerent group and those who were more level headed. Finally, wise counsels prevailed. Big Bill Ferris was elected to accompany the doctor. The team was hitched to the sleigh. One last objection was raised.

"Doc, how do we know what these murtherin villains will do to you men? You know you'd be no match for a crowd of them."

"Boys, I'm not a bit afraid. They'll think I am visiting one of their people who is ill. They'll not interfere with me, I am sure. Why you know boys, some of those fellows wouldn't be alive today, but for me."

Just as the sleigh was about to leave, Pete Small rushed up with a musket and thrust it into the doctor's hands. "There Doctor, take that, it's a brand new one and it's loaded, and if one of those dastards says an oncivil word to you, why give him hell, and here's some bullets and some powder in case you need them."

So the doctor and big Bill drove off. But what were these four hundred men to do? There was nothing to do but wait. Time drags wearily under such circumstances, and in a short time some of the crowd became restless.

"Isn't it time they were back?" said one.

"What's keeping them so long," said another.

"Why what are you fellows talking about," said a third, "they haven't had time to get down there yet, let alone get back. Have a little patience, and a little sense."

Two o'clock arrived. Few of these men carried a watch,

but the few who did so were called upon to declare the time every few minutes. When three o'clock arrived and no sign of the travellers, there was a strong movement among the men.

"How do we know what became of Doc and Bill? They may be dead. They may be lyin' on the roadside wounded. Here there are four hundred of us standin' idle, and doin' nothin'. I say let's march."

This appeal received a favourable response from many. One of the most highly respected men in the community however, spoke up quietly but emphatically, "Boys, take it easy, you know the roads are heavy. It is too soon to expect them back here. I have been figuring this out. I calculate if all goes well they should be back by four o'clock. If not, then we would have some cause for fear. Now boys, I propose that we wait as patiently as we can until four. If by that time Bill and the Doc are not back here, safe and sound, we'll go down and if those fellows have touched a hair of their heads, we'll take it out of their hides. What do you say men?"

"Hear, hear," "That's good sense" came from various sections of the crowd. "Very well then, four o'clock will be the deadline."

The crowd was quiet after this. Three-fifteen, three-thirty, still no signs of the travellers. The tension grew, the crowd became very still, all eyes were strained to the south and east. The watches were consulted again and again. At three forty-five, one of the younger men pointing his finger said: "What's that yonder way down the road there?" "I can't see anything," said another. "But I do," said the first. "It's a black thing, and it wasn't there a little while ago." Others confirmed his statement.

"There is something, and by golly it's moving. It is, sure enough! And it looks like horses. It is! It's them, hurrah, hurrah!"

Soon the doctor and Bill drove into the midst of the crowd and received a hilarious welcome.

"Well Doc, what's the news?" from a score of tongues.

"News, why there is no news. The people of Ajala are all asleep in their beds. We didn't see a light in a single house, did we Bill?"

"Nope, nary a one, all the life we saw was a few dogs that barked at us as we passed by."

"Now boys," said the doctor, "you can all go home and Pete, here's your gun and your ammunition. We didn't need any of it, but thank you just the same."

"Aye, it was a quare wild night," remarked old George Rutledge, as he finished the story. "We were all pretty tired and sleepy. Some had a long way to go through the bush, and do you know Mr. Coburn, some of the boys weren't too well plazed. They had come for a fight and were ready for it. But most of us were satisfied. I have often thought since, what a mercy of God that Dr. Robinson was home that night. But for him I have no doubt these men would have marched down into Ajala, and then what would have happened? God only knows. One thing is sure. Hatred and bitterness would have been created that night, that would have lasted for many a day." Then with a laugh, "It's a bit funny too when you think of it. All these people in Ajala sound asleep, never dreamin' how close they were to war."

I asked the old man, "But Mr. Rutledge, how in the world did such a rumour get started, who started it?"

"Aye, my boy that's the mystery. That was 1866, this is 1893, twenty-seven years ago and no one knows to this day who was responsible. Those that did it, whoever they were, just kept quiet, and the authorities didn't bother to search it out. I suppose as no harm came to anyone they thought it better just to lave it alone."

3

ALGOMA LIFE

1. *Oatmeals, Philistines and Methodists*

ABOUT thirty-five miles south-east of what is now the thriving
city of Sault Ste. Marie, there is a tract of good farming
land. Part of it was settled by a group of Highland Scotch
people, who soon after their arrival established a Presbyterian Church. In that church, for many years, services
in Gaelic (the language of the Garden of Eden, they
claimed), as well as in English were held. They were
conducted on the old, orthodox Presbyterian model. No
"kist o' whistles" in the shape of an organ was allowed
within the sacred precincts of their little kirk. They sang
no hymns, only psalms and paraphrases, in very slow time,
and led by a Precentor. This Precentor sat up near the
pulpit. By the aid of a tuning fork, he found the right
pitch for the tune he intended to use for each psalm or
paraphrase. For several years this church was ministered
to by a man of very narrow views. He had little regard for
any church but the Presbyterian, and as for the Methodists
they were almost beneath his contempt. He claimed that
hymns like Wesley's "Jesus Lover of My Soul" were the
sheerest blasphemy.

In course of time, however, some of the younger generation came in contact with church life in the Soo and other
places. They wanted an organ, and music of a wider variety.
A few of the older generation supported the young people,
but the minister, most of the elders and a majority of the
congregation clung to the old ways. Then came the rebel-
lion followed by a disruption. Opposite the church there
stood a hall belonging to a secret society. The rebels rented
this hall and began holding services. The Presbytery in this
case did an unusual thing in giving its sanction to the new
congregation. For years, at MacLennan, a hamlet consisting
of a store, a blacksmith shop and one or two houses, these
two Presbyterian congregations carried on. The two
congregations acquired names at first applied as terms of
derision, but gradually accepted and used to designate the
two groups. The older group were called the Oatmeals and
the newer group the Philistines.

Finally the old minister died and the Presbytery seized
the opportunity to effect a reconciliation. A compromise
was arranged. The singing would be led by an organ, but
nothing but psalms and paraphrases would be sung. This
condition prevailed for several years.

About the same time as these Highlanders arrived,
another group came from the counties of Huron and Bruce
in Ontario. These people were a mixture, English, Irish and
a few Scotch, but most of them Canadian born. A large
proportion of them were Methodists. A leader among them
was one Thomas Nott. He was a man of sound judgment
and devout spirit, an old-fashioned Methodist. Under his
leadership a Methodist class was organized which met first
in private homes, then in a school house and later in a little
frame church which the Methodists erected. It was situated
about a mile from MacLennan. The Tarbutt appointment
as it was called was attached, first to the Garden River
Mission, later Port Finlay and finally to the Echo Bay field.
Though their churches were only a mile apart, there was

no fraternization between the Methodists of Tarbutt and
the Presbyterians of MacLennan. Union services or inter-
changes of pulpits were never thought of.

The Methodist field had from the beginning been served
by unordained students who were lacking in experience
and who usually served but one year. There was therefore
little continuity about the work. Thomas Nott was like a
father to the "boys" as he called them. He was ever ready
to give them wise, kindly advice, and if really necessary, a
good sound scolding, but woe to anyone who criticized any
of these lads in his hearing. His home was open to them
at any hour, day or night. As it was before the days of
modern church finance, it was the duty of the steward to
call upon all the members and adherents of the church once
a quarter, receive their contributions to the preacher's salary
and pay over the same at the Quarterly Board meeting. I
happened to be making a pastoral call at a house one day,
when Mr. Nott who was the steward called for the "quar-
terage." In his own unvarnished way he gave these folk
a wonderful talk on stewardship. He told them that they
really owned nothing, that all they had was the gift of God.
The strength with which they worked their land was from
Him. "What good," he asked, "would your work and mine
be if the Almighty forgot to send the rain and the sunshine?
It's surely as little as we can do to give a little of all that
He has given us to help carry on His work."

Mr. Nott told me and laughed in the telling, about once
when he was out collecting for one of my predecessors.
"You know, Coburn," he said, "he was a mighty weak
preacher. It was all I could do to sit and listen to him
myself but he was a good, sincere boy and of course, I
wouldn't let anyone say a word against him. Among others,
I called on Tommy Higgins. Tommy, not a member of the
Church, was a little wild, but came to church quite often
and all in all wasn't such a bad chap. When I asked Tommy
for a contribution he said, "Aw now Mr. Nott, you

wouldn't ask a fellow to pay for such lame preaching as yon fellow hands out." Mr. Nott replied, "Oh, but Tommy, this money is for the Lord's cause you know." "Well, if it's for the Lord I suppose I'll have to give you a dollar but if you had a decent preacher there I'd give you two."

Christmas day, the year of my pastorate there, was a Saturday. Mr. Nott's family insisted that my wife and I spend the day with them. (My wife was the first minister's wife on the field and this family made quite a fuss over her.) All the children and grandchildren of the Nott family within reach were on hand. We were a jolly party of twenty-five or thirty. Roast turkey, plum pudding, mince pies and numerous most delicious eatables were in abundance. Mr. and Mrs. Nott were determined that their guests would do full justice to everything. In the night I became very sick, and on getting up in the morning, it was certainly "the day after the night before." I had three services that day and a drive of over twenty miles through the snow. My morning appointment was at a little church called Laird. The people at Laird were the most exacting as to the pastor's services of any on the field, but were less willing to pay their fair share of the expenses. Mr. Nott had many a tussle with the representatives from Laird at the Quarterly Board meetings. When I at last managed to get dressed and downstairs, Mr. Nott looked me over and said: "Well, young man, you don't look as if you'd be a whirlwind in the pulpit this morning; feel kind of squeamish, don't you?" I had to admit that his analysis of the situation was correct.

"Well, I'll tell you what we'll do. You get yourself in shape to preach here at Tarbutt this afternoon, and I'll go and take the service at Laird—Mother, get me my white shirt." While he was being arrayed in his best garments, he turned to me and said, "Where's that verse in the Bible about Moses lifting up the serpent in the wilderness?" I turned up John 3 and read: "As Moses lifted up the serpent in the wilderness even so must the Son of Man be lifted up."

"That's the thing," he said, "and I'll tell them that the best way to lift up the Son of Man is to pay their fair share of the preacher's salary."

The exegesis was certainly novel and the application somewhat startling. On my next visit to Laird, the leading official told me that when I found it necessary to send them a local preacher, they would prefer one of the other men rather than Mr. Nott.

A couple of years after Mr. Nott's death, some years later, the Mission Board of the Presbyterian and Methodist churches decided that they would no longer support two home missionaries in territory that could be effectively served by one. Some time before Church Union of 1925, a general scheme of amalgamation was effected, under which the congregations of MacLennan and Tarbutt were united. That meant, of course, that the ban on hymns had to be lifted, but as most of the old Oatmeals by this time had been gathered to their fathers, there was no serious difficulty.

Then on June 10, 1925, Oatmeals, Philistines and Methodists and their descendants became members of the United Church at MacLennan. As such they worship to this day. Only a very few now have any memory of the divisions and rivalries of earlier days. The pioneer Presbyterians and Methodists builded better than they knew.

2. *From the Heart of London to the Wilds of Algoma*

In 1897 there came to Algoma a family from the heart of old London. John Cowan was a bookkeeper. His family consisted of his wife, a son in his early twenties, another in his late teens and three younger daughters. One Sunday afternoon the people in Tarbutt church were somewhat startled to see these seven persons enter the church. As the service had begun they slipped quietly into a back seat which happened to be vacant. From my point of vantage in the pulpit, I had a better opportunity of sizing up the newcomers than had most of the congregation. They were dressed a little differently. I noticed that they joined heartily in the hymns and that they appeared to follow the service with more than average interest. At that church, as in most rural Methodist churches at that time, a short class meeting was held at the close of the public service. For this latter service, only members of the church usually remained, though any who desired were free to do so. The strangers remained. After several members had, according to usual custom, related their experience, Mr. Cowan arose and said: "My dear friends, my family and I esteem it a great privilege to be here this afternoon. A few days ago we arrived from England. We have been life-long Methodists. I do not see how we could have been happy in our new home if there were no Methodist chapel for us to attend. To hear the Gospel preached as we have been used to hearing it and to have a part in this class meeting is a great joy to us. We are strangers in a strange land, but here in this chapel we feel wonderfully at home. We understand that this chapel is the nearest one to our home—seven miles from here." Addressing me, he continued: "If you sir, and your good people are willing to receive us, we shall be glad to make this place our spiritual home. We will welcome the fellowship of those who, like ourselves, love God and his Church."

The simple, warm-hearted farmers of that little congregation needed no urging to give the strangers a cordial welcome. At the close of the service they were at once surrounded. Everybody shook hands and some of the older people spoke kindly words of greeting. I learned that they had driven to service in a lumber wagon (a vehicle without springs). It was a tedious trip but they declared that they didn't in the least mind the discomfort.

As soon as I could I paid them a pastoral visit. Mr. Cowan informed me that he was a bookkeeper and that he had held a very good position in the "City," meaning old London.

"But," said he, "we wished to give our children a better chance than they could ever have in England. Not much chance sir, at 'ome for young people to better their position. My good wife and I had cherished this ambition since the children were small. We 'eard of Canada, a great new land where all men were equal, no upper, middle and lower classes. We also 'eard that land was cheap. So, during the years, we saved all we could. I invested our savings and had a bit of good luck there. So, sir, with a few 'undred pounds we set out, and 'ere we are."

"How did you find your way to this precise spot?" I inquired.

"We got as far as Toronto, and fell in with a land agent who told us of a fine farm of one 'undred and sixty acres that could be bought cheaply and with a small down payment. The amount he mentioned was well within our means. A 'undred and sixty acres, why Mr. Coburn none of us ever dreamed we would ever own that much land—our very, very own. I tell you sir, we were so excited we just couldn't wait to get here."

"But you surely didn't buy the property without seeing it," I suggested.

"Well you see, Mr. Coburn, it was this way. We would have preferred to see the place first of course, but the gentleman said as how another person was after the place and that he could not hold it for us longer than until the next day. He explained to us that there was a house all ready for us to move into and a barn on the place. We felt it was too good to miss. So we paid the money, and got a bill of sale. Come, I'd like to show you over my 'estite'!" He bubbled over with pride and enthusiasm, but I felt sick at heart. There was some good land, but most of it was rock

and a steep hill that could not be cultivated. A former settler
had tried to make a home of the place but had abandoned
it. The house was a poor one and the barn was in a bad
condition of disrepair. The prospect was a gloomy one.
An experienced farmer would have had a hard struggle to
make a living for a family on that farm. What was to
become of those innocent folk from the heart of London?
I didn't know. I would like to have got my hands or rather
my tongue on that scoundrel of a land agent. These people
had been robbed. It is no credit to Canada, that many
decent folk from across the sea, having come to its shores
with high hopes of making a comfortable home have been
fleeced by rascally land agents, implement dealers and other
parasites. Rarely during my whole life have I felt as angry
as I did that day. With some effort I restrained my wrath.
To have told them the truth would have done no good.
They were here. They had at least a roof over their heads.
They had nowhere else to go. Personally I could do little
to help them, but I secured the help of one who could.
My good friend Thomas Nott, the leading official of the
Tarbutt church, was a successful farmer, a man of shrewd
common sense, and withal a man of the kindliest disposition.
Being an Englishman himself I knew he would be interested
in the Cowans. I laid the whole case before him. He was
able to give advice and counsel that was helpful and I am
suspicious that, on occasion, more than advice passed from
Thomas Nott to John Cowan.

At any rate, to my surprise they stayed for some years
on that farm. The boys spent the winters in the lumber
woods and also earned some cash helping neighbouring
farmers in the busy seasons. The older girl secured a position
as maid in a home in a town some miles away. Mr. and
Mrs. Cowan toiled patiently and hard, early and late. Life
for them was one long struggle. It was marvellous, how
they adapted themselves to Algoma conditions. As far as I
could learn, no one ever heard a word of complaint from

them. It is just common folk like the Cowans who have gone to the ends of the earth, faced all kinds of difficulty without fear, refused to be beaten by any complication of adverse circumstances, have finally won out and made England the heart of an Empire upon which for many years the sun never set.

In connection with the near tragedy of the Cowan situation there were two humorous incidents.

When the elder Cowan was showing me over his "estite" of one hundred and sixty acres, and telling me of his plans and hopes, he confided in me that one matter was giving them a little difficulty. It was the cow, pronounced by Mr. Cowan kauow. "For some reason," said he, "she won't stand still to be milked, sometimes she gives very little. We bought her from a neighbour and everyone says she is quiet and easy to milk. Maybe she feels a bit stringe."

I felt the poor bossy was the one in need of sympathy in this instance. After being milked by one who thoroughly understood the business (and there is a real knack in milking) to have one of these ex-Londoners make the attempt would be enough to try the patience of any respectable cow. My wonder was that they succeeded in getting any milk at all.

"How have you managed Mr. Cowan?" I asked.

"Come, I'll show you. It is just about milking time."

He took me to a fence, that was built around a small plot of land called the garden. In this fence there was the cow standing half way through the gateway. The younger Cowan boy stood at her head, the younger girl immediately behind her. Each had a switch in hand. The older girl sat on a stool and was milking the cow.

"That is the only way we can get any milk at all Mr. Coburn. You see the gateposts prevent her moving sidewise, Billy prevents her going forward, Emily prevents her backing up, while Polly milks her."

Nearing the close of my pastorate, I spent a night at the home of my good friend John Irwin. John had a small farm and supplemented his income from it in various ways. One of these ways was by acting as an agent for a nursery. It was his duty to take orders for young treelets and deliver them to customers. In the morning, John said to me, "Say, Mr. Coburn, how would you like to go out and see the Cowans today? I have to deliver some young trees in their neighbourhood. I would be glad of the company and you could make a pastoral call, what do you say?"

"That will be fine, John. I really ought to pay them a farewell visit before I leave and I might not get another chance to do so."

So in due time we set out. We arrived at the home of the Cowans about four o'clock in the afternoon. Mrs. Cowan insisted that we have a cup of tea. She seated us at the table and brought out a very dainty and beautiful tea set— one of the treasured possessions she had brought with her "from 'ome." Probably it was a wedding present.

The cup, saucer and plate were quite small. John and I sat opposite each other. When John sat down, he took a look at his plate and then looked at me in such a way as nearly upset my gravity. John had a great sense of humour and was chuck full of mischief. I knew exactly what was in his mind. Here was this great husky farmer who always sat down to a good, big plate—well filled and soon emptied, and before him was a wee piece of dainty china that would hold only two or three bites. But the worst was yet to come. Mrs. Cowan filled our cups, then set down the tea pot on the table, and carefully pulled over it a very pretty tea cosy. I saw a look of utter amazement on John's face. He had never seen a thing like that before.

After we started home and had got out of sight and sound of the house, John threw back his head and roared.

"Why John, what's the matter?" I asked.

"Matter," said he. "Whoever saw people eat off wee

things like that. Do they call them things plates? And then the tea pot. Say Coburn, was that old Cowan's night cap she put on the tea pot?" It was my turn then to laugh. In fact I had several good laughs before we reached John's house. The ways of these folk from the heart of London amid Algoma wilds and the attitude of my friend John, rugged son of Canada's back woods were equally amusing.

4

A PIONEER CASE IN CHILD WELFARE WORK

AT ECHO BAY, Algoma, I was confronted with one of the most distressing cases I have ever met with. Jack Bourne, whose wife had been dead for several years, had two children, a boy and girl apparently about 12 and 10 years of age respectively. Though living about a mile and a half from a school, neither attended and neither could read nor write. As I visited my people in their homes some of them told me most dreadful stories of the conditions in the Bourne house and the filth and indecency in which these children were being brought up.

As the only minister resident in the community I felt I could not tolerate such things. At that time there was little machinery for the care of destitute or neglected children in Ontario. A Child Protection Act had been passed and Mr. J. J. Kelso had been appointed Provincial officer a short time before, but there were no local Children's Aid Societies or shelters. Child Welfare work was spasmodic and ineffective.

I took a friend with me and visited the Bourne home. We found the children alone in the house, and though it was winter, there was no fire. The boy's clothes were so ragged that if he had appeared on the street of any town, he would have been arrested for indecent exposure. The girl had some old garments and rags pulled over her. Her dress, if it was a dress, seemed to have no shape. The boy had evidently tried to put all the clothing on her to keep her warm. The one redeeming feature of the whole situation was the gentle care, and almost maternal solicitude of this rude boy for his sister. Both children were exceedingly dirty. The house was the filthiest human habitation I had ever seen. I had visited homes in the slums of Toronto but had never encountered anything like this. The children took us to their father, who was in the bush chopping wood.

"Good day, Mr. Bourne, my name is Coburn. I am the Methodist minister at Echo Bay. I have come to see you about this boy and girl of yours. They tell me your wife died some years ago, and that you have had to care for these children ever since. That's a tough job for a man, to be both father and mother to a growing boy and girl. You know we men are a bit awkward at work like that. We don't make a very good fist of it. Now, Mr. Bourne, I am greatly interested in children. I am a member of an orphanage board that cares for boys and girls who have lost one or both of their parents. I can arrange to have these children fed, clothed and educated so as to be able to take their place in the world without a cent of expense to you. What do you say?"

"If you and all the other —— Methodists would mind your own damn business it would suit me. These kids are mine, and I'll do what I damn please with them."

"No, Mr. Bourne you can't do just as you please even with a dog. In Sault Ste. Marie last week a man was fined for abusing a dog. The law of Canada protects these children. Your neglect and abuse of them constitutes a crime punishable by three years in penitentiary. All I have to do is to have you brought to court and sent down; then these children become wards of the Province and will be cared for. But I don't want to send you to prison. I came out here to help you. I have made you a good offer and if you had the interest of these children at heart, you would gladly accept. But if you are stubborn you will compel me to take the hard way. Think it over, man, and let me know if you change your mind. I will do nothing for a few days. I have no desire to be anything but a friend to you, but be sure of one thing, no children will be subjected to abuse and neglect in any community in which I live if I can prevent it."

"Go to hell, you and your damn Methodists. I tell you I'll do as I like with these kids, they're mine. You and the law—you can't do nothin' to me. Go ahead and do your damndest."

Now, as I have already said, there was no local Children's Aid Society. There was no lawyer or other person informed on such matters within reach. There was, however, in one of my congregations a lady whose husband had recently died, who was a Justice of the Peace. I borrowed from her, her husband's copy of the Criminal Code and the latest Revised Statutes of Ontario. I studied diligently and found that under the terms of recent legislation Mr. Kelso, the Provincial officer, had authority to appoint persons to represent him in any case. I wrote him fully and received a very kind letter in reply, appointing me his agent; so I had official status. One day I visited the home of one of my church members who was a Justice of the Peace and swore out information against Bourne in the terms of the Criminal Code. A few days later this J.P.'s son delivered a bundle of papers at my home. They proved to be the summonses for Bourne and the various witnesses. With them was a note stating that the J.P. could find no constable who would serve the papers. Bourne had openly threatened to shoot anyone who attempted to do so. The worthy J.P. sent the papers to me, a mere Methodist preacher, and said if I wanted them served I would have to get them served myself.

It was rather a strange situation. However, I had a little .32 revolver which, on the advice and with the consent of a magistrate, I had carried for a time on one of my student fields where certain of "the baser sort" had made threats against me. I planned to ask this J.P. to swear me in as a special constable and then with a friend and my trusty six shooter go down, beard the lion in his den and vindicate the law. That, happily, proved to be unnecessary.

Two members of my church from the farthest appointment called in one evening on their way home from the Soo. We persuaded them to stay for supper. At the table I told them of our difficulty. One of them said: "Well Mr. Coburn, I can help you. I am a district constable and I am not afraid of the old reprobate. A man like that is always a coward. I'll serve the papers for you."

I thanked him and told him he would be rendering a real service in the interest not only of these neglected children but of law and order generally.

After supper I went over to the Post Office for the mail (in the local general store). The place was full of men and lo, among them was none other than Jack Bourne himself. I rushed back to the house, got the papers and said to my friend: "Come on, John, our bird has flown right into a trap. Bourne is at the Post Office." In a few minutes the papers were served and as Bourne had no gun there was no shooting.

The trial was held in the Orange Hall. The whole countryside was present. Two Justices of the Peace presided. One of them had never sat on a case before. The other one knew very little about law or legal proceedure. In fact they relied on me to tell them what to do. In spite of many hours of study of the borrowed law books there were many things I did not know. I explained to their "Worships" that in this case the accused had the right to elect whether he would be tried summarily by them or by a judge and jury. If he chose the latter they must hold a preliminary hearing and if the evidence warranted commit him for such trial. One of the J.P.'s solemnly arose and said: "John Bourne stand up." John stood. The J.P. then read the charge and said: "Will you be tried by us or will you elect?"

"Let her go Galliger, I might as well be tried here as anywhere," responded the accused. The trial then proceeded. One feature that would have amused a legal man was that we proceeded to try the wretched creature without asking him to plead guilty or not guilty. (The Justices evidently did not know it ought to be done, and I had so many details of the case to keep in mind I did not notice the omission.) As complainant I had to act as prosecutor. I spent four hours examining witnesses. Here I had unlooked for difficulty. The people who had given me information so freely and urged action did not seem to know nearly so much in the witness box. It puzzled me until later I learned that Bourne had threatened to burn out anyone who gave evidence against him. A jurist would have been horrified at the proceedings. I examined and *cross-examined* my own witnesses. I did not then know it was against the rules—neither did the Justices, nor the accused, nor anybody else at that court.

In spite of all the difficulties, sufficient evidence was adduced to show that over a period of years these children had suffered from neglect, abuse and immoral teaching, and had lived in conditions of indescribable filth. One man told of visiting the home one night on business. Bourne was away, the two children, only little folk then were alone in the house. Though it was below zero weather, the fire had gone out and Bourne had left them no wood to carry on. When the man entered the house one child crawled out of the oven of the cook stove and the other from underneath it. They had tried to get the benefit of any heat from the defunct fire.

At this stage an old man, Bob Rush by name, came forward and asked leave to address the court. He was a

Quaker now living in the Soo, but a former resident of
Echo Bay who knew all the parties involved. He held the
position of Provincial constable though not on continuous
duty. I found out afterwards that he had taken Bourne
aside and addressed him: "Say Jack you may not know it,
but you are in the devil of a mess. This darn preacher has
you where the hair is short. You'll go down stream as sure
as fate. But I don't think he's a half bad fellow if you take
him right. In fact I don't think he's after you at all. It's
the kids he's after and he's going to get 'em—mark my words.
Now if you'll let me I'll speak a word for you and see what
can be done."

So Bob came forward. He well knew the limitations of
the two men on the bench. He made a very wise suggestion: "Your Worships," he said, "this is a very ticklish case.
Neither you nor Mr. Coburn have had experience in
handling such. You are all doing your best no doubt, but
I suggest that all parties agree to take this whole case up
to Judge Johnston of the Soo. He is a good judge and a
kindly man who will do the best for all concerned." The
proposal delighted me. I could see difficulties ahead—
certain technicalities which I did not fully understand, and
which I was quite sure the court did not understand at all.
I gave a somewhat hesitant assent fearing that if I appeared
eager Bourne might object. He consented too. I insisted,
however, that some decent provision be made for the children in the meantime. Dan Alton, one of the substantial
farmers present, an adherent of my church, rose and said:
"The children are welcome to come to my house and stay.
My misssus will be glad to take care of them. Then when
youse is all ready I will drive youse all up to the Soo in my
sleigh." This was most satisfactory. The magistrates then
asked me if they should dismiss the case. "Oh no, Your
Worships if you do that we are out of court. I suggest that
you adjourn the case for say two weeks. By that time we
will have visited the Judge and then can act accordingly."

"Court adjourned for two weeks."

The children were moved to their temporary home where they had for the first time in their lives a good bath and were clad in warm garments. They were taken to a church social at which there was the usual abundance of good things to eat. The youngsters fell to with a will. The next day they developed severe colds and suffered from badly upset stomachs. Bourne declared that the damned interfering Coburn and his blasted Methodists were killing his children. However, a good dose of salts and liberal outward applications of goose grease and turpentime induced rapid recovery. On a bright cold morning in January, Bourne, the children and I packed ourselves in straw and quilts in Dan Alton's sleigh and started for the Soo, 22 miles away, Dan himself driving. An appointment with His Honour, Judge Johnson, had been previously made.

On arriving at the Soo, instead of going to the Judge's chambers, as agreed, Bourne made for McFadden's law office. Now Moses McFadden, the senior member of the firm, a genial warm-hearted Irishman, had some time before written me a letter pointing out that Bourne was a poor man and urging me not to expect too much of him. I had replied giving him the main facts in the case. When I saw what Bourne was up to I followed him. On our arrival, McFadden told Bourne to sit down (in the outer office) and took me into his private office.

"Now Mr. Coburn," he said, "please understand this. I'm not going to interfere with any good Christian work you are trying to do for these children. Bourne came to me and told me you were trying to send him to prison. I thought perhaps you, a young fellow from the city, just out of college might be expecting things a bit too spic and span in this rough country and with these folk, most of whom are pretty poor. But from your letter and information from other sources I am satisfied you are doing the right thing. When I wrote that letter for Bourne, I charged him $2.00

and then gave it back to him to buy something for the
children and told him to go home and get things fixed up. If
I had charged the old scoundrel a good fancy fee perhaps
he would have taken my advice. Well, come along. The
judge is waiting for us."

Judge Johnston received us in his chambers. I stated
the case. He called the boy over to him. The boy answered
quite shortly.

"Haven't you any manners?" said the judge.

The poor boy didn't know what he meant.

"How old are you?"

"Fourteen."

"Better say sir, hadn't you?"

"All right, sir, if you like."

"Can you read and write?"

"No, sir."

"Been to school?"

"Once."

"Once, what do you mean?"

"I went one day a long time ago."

Turning to me the judge asked: "How far is the school
away from their home?"

"Hardly a mile and a half, Your Honour."

"Bourne, you ought be horse-whipped. To have two
children within a mile and a half of a school and not have
them atttend and to have a boy of fourteen unable to read
and write is a scandal. I was articled to a lawyer when
I was only a little older than this boy. By the way Bourne,
where did you come from?"

"County of Huron."

"Yes, near Goderich wasn't it?"

"Yes sir."

"I thought so. I come from there, too. Was your name
Bourne in Huron County?" Bourne fidgeted from one foot
to the other, looked down at the floor, then up to the ceiling.

"Come, come, answer my question. Was your name Bourne when you lived in Huron?"

"No."

"What was it?"

"Wright."

"Yes, Jack Wright, I recognized you the minute you came in the door." Then the Judge turned very sternly to me:

"No, Mr. Coburn, I'll have nothing to do with your case. If what you have sworn to in that information is true, and from what has appeared here, I fear it is, then this man is a criminal. Canadian law says that such a man should go to prison for three years. That is the place for him. You go back to the magistrates, push your case, and if you succeed let them sentence him. Then come back to me and we will dispose of the children."

This was all for effect to thoroughly scare Bourne, for later the Judge proceeded to do the very thing he said he wouldn't do.

McFadden and I both interceded for him. I declared I had no desire to send him down, but wanted the children taken care of. After much persuasion the judge appeared to relent and asked Bourne if he had any proposition to make. Bourne stated that a farmer named McBain had agreed to board the children at a certain price.

"What do you say to that, Coburn?" said the judge. "Do you know McBain? Is he a suitable person to have charge of the children?"

"Yes, Your Honour, I know McBain. He and his good wife are estimable people. But McBain is a comparatively poor man, a hard working farmer. He has children of his own. He couldn't afford to keep these children for nothing. I am afraid as soon as this case blows over Bourne will simply quit paying and the children will be back in that filthy den again."

"Well, we'll see if we can fix that. Bourne, are you

willing to sign a written agreement to board your children at McBain's and to pay the specified amount monthly?"

"Yes sir, I'll do that."

"Now, Mr. McFadden, you take Mr. Coburn to your office and draw up an agreement as binding as words can make it and I suggest that you, Mr. Coburn, take the agreement home with you, get both McBain and Bourne to sign it with you as witness. Then you can report to the magistrates and you can withdraw the case or they can dispose of it any way you and they think best. And you, Bourne, or Wright, you may think yourself lucky if you get out of this mess as easily as is proposed. This minister is a real friend to both you and your children. And don't you forget to make those payments as agreed. I warn you if you appear before me again in this connection I will deal sternly with you."

The lawyer drew the agreement. I received McBain's signature but my friend Bourne refused to sign and boasted to everyone that he had trimmed me before the judge. But, poor fool, he was not out of the woods. The Magistrate's Court was only adjourned. When it met I stated the facts, and pointed out that notwithstanding the prisoner's election they had the right to send the case to the District Court. I therefore moved that on the basis of evidence already received they commit the accused for trial before a judge and jury at the next court of competent jurisdiction. There being no constable near, the question arose as to arresting the accused and conveying him to the gaol in the Soo. The court sat on a Saturday afternoon. I was going to the Soo on the evening train to preach on Sunday and at Evangelistic services the week following. The magistrates made out the warrant for his arrest and committal asking that I take it to the Soo and send a constable down to make the arrest.

The gaoler, Mr. Dawson, was one of the pillars of the Methodist Church. At the close of the service one evening, he came up to me laughing and said:

"I have a friend of yours visiting at my house just now. But say, Mr. Coburn, he is without doubt the filthiest human being I ever had charge of, and I've had to deal with some rum ones. We stripped him and hung all his clothes out on a line. This zero weather ought to do something to all that livestock. We gave him a good hot bath and I put two of the prisoners on him with a flesh brush and wash cloths and lots of soap. I think we got his body fairly clean but his hair and whiskers are just matted. I am sure that man has had no bath for years and a comb is something his hair is a complete stranger to."

Next day Moses McFadden's young brother and law partner came to see me. He said:

"Bourne sent for me as soon as he was arrested, but I let him wait until today. I went to the gaol and said to him: 'Bourne, my brother and I are willing to do anything for your kids for nothing, glad of the opportunity, but not a darn thing will we do for you without pay.' Well the old rascal pulled a ten dollar bill out of his pocket and gave it to me. Believe me, Mr Coburn, it was so dirty that it was stiff and the smell of it would knock you down. I took it to a drug store and asked them to give me two fives for a ten. I thought they could disinfect it. Of course, we must defend him and save him from going to prison if we can, but remember what my brother said to you stands. Anything we can do for the children will be gladly done."

I explained to the lawyer that I had no wish to send his client to prison and that if he would sign the agreement and transfer his children to McBain's home and keep up his payments he had nothing to fear from me. McFadden said he would certainly advise him that he must do that. Later we arranged with the Crown Attorney to let him out on his own bail, half hoping that he would slip over to the United States. But he did not do so. On my return to Echo Bay Jack lost no time in hunting me up and getting the papers signed. I thereupon withdrew the charges against him. The children were moved to McBain's home and started to school.

If this story were fiction one could give it a happy ending. Sad to tell, the end was not happy. I remained at Echo Bay about six months after the events here related, then I was moved to a mission field in Muskoka four hundred miles away. As long as I was in the neighbourhood Bourne made his monthly payments and all went well. Soon after I left, I am told, he ceased to pay, and, as I feared, the children were returned to him. No one in the community seemed to have the courage to bring the matter before Judge Johnston. When the unfortunate girl was about eighteen years of age she died in childbirth. Before her death she admitted to a neighbour that the child was Bourne's.

So all our work seemed to go for nothing. However, it was cases such as this that stirred the consciences of the people of Ontario and their representatives in the legislature to enact several pieces of useful and effective child welfare legislation. Since then the Children's Protection Act has been amended and greatly strengthened, the Mother's Allowances Act, the Act for the Protection of Children of Unmarried Parents, and some Child Labour Legislation have been passed. There is a well organized and strongly staffed Child Welfare Department in the Provincial Government. In nearly every County and District there is a Children's Aid Society with a comfortable shelter for the care of its wards. The Big Brother and Big Sister associations are rendering splendid service. Juvenile Courts are dealing with cases of child neglect and delinquency with an understanding and efficiency unknown in the days of the Bourne episode. There is abundance of legislation on the statute books and ample machinery for dealing speedily and effectually with any social cases anywhere in Ontario. Unfortunately the fundamental social and economic conditions that produce many of the cases still remain.

5

A COUNTRY PARSON

1. *A Village Blacksmith's Interpretation of a Sermon*

Two YEARS of my early ministry were spent on a rather difficult mission field in Muskoka. The land was very rocky. Practically all the valuable timber had been cut. Most of the people of initiative and general ability to get on, had moved. Those left behind were for the most part narrow in their outlook and somewhat hard to work with.

There was one man who was not a native. He was the village blacksmith, an Englishman. John had come of good stock in the old land. His mother had died in his early childhood. His father having married again, John and the new mistress of the home could not "hit it off." So John ran away. As a result he received no schooling, in fact could not read or write beyond the signing of his name. Yet he was intelligent far beyond his neighbours. He took a daily paper and when the mail arrived someone in the house had to drop everything and read John the news. He was better posted on public affairs than many who had enjoyed superior advantages. My visits to his shop to have Dolly shod or some repairs made to my "rig" were always interesting and revealing. Frequently John wanted to talk about the sermon of the previous Sunday. I discovered that the sermons on which I had expended the most brain sweat were those in which my friend was most deeply interested.

My term at this place was nearly ended when I brought Dolly to the shop to be shod by John for the last time.

"So you're goin' to leave us?" John asked.

"Yes, that's the order now."

"Well, I'm sorry and I'm glad. I'm glad for your sake. It'll be a poor place they have sent you to if it isn't better than this. I'll miss you and Dolly, though, comin' to the shop. What like is the fellow that is to come in your place?"

"Oh, he's a fine chap. I went to College with him and you'll find him splendid."

"Well, he'd better be. Any fellow that comes round here stuck up and puttin' on airs'll get small notice from me. Say I guess you think you've had a rum time these two years. Don't forget no preacher has ever stayed more nor two years and some got out at the end of one."

Then after a few contemplative puffs at an old black pipe and a good vigorous spit he went on: "I was just thinkin', I've been here sixteen years, I've seen several of these here parsons come and go. I really think you've come through on the whole easier than any of them. Do you know why?"

"No," I said, "I'd be glad to know."

"It was that first sermon you preached, don't you remember?"

I did remember. On my first Sunday appearance, knowing the history of the place and the difficulties my predecessors had experienced, I had spoken to the congregation quite plainly. In fact in as kindly fashion as possible, I laid down the law to them.

"Yes," said John, as he worked the bellows of his forge, "You bet, you just stood up in the pulpit and told them you didn't give a damn for anybody." Then with a chuckle: "By golly, that fixed them proper."

2. *A Gamble for a Woman's Life*

When I went from Echo Bay in Algoma to a mission field in Muskoka I found that though the Muskoka district had been settled for a much longer time, the people here too, still suffered from a lack of medical care. The population was sparse, the roads very rough. In some cases a doctor would have to make a round of sixty miles to visit a patient. The messenger who went for him would have to do the same as there were neither telephone nor telegraph facilities. We were in a particularly favoured position as our parsonage was only fourteen miles from town. In case of emergency that was quite far enough.

Through the insistence of my mother, I brought with me a supply of simple remedies for colds and such like. In some way the people found out that I had a clinical thermometer and that I knew how to use it and to take a pulse. Some of them had a most exaggerated idea of my knowledge along medical lines and in cases of illness frequently sent for me. If it was some simple thing that I understood I would do what I could for them, but if it appeared to be serious I would insist that a doctor be sent for at once.

At this place there lived a fine family, leaders in all phases of church work and close friends of the folks in the parsonage. One evening about five o'clock, the youngest child, a girl of about ten years of age came into the parsonage crying.

"Why Jennie," said my wife, "what's the matter dear?"

"Oh Mrs. Coburn, Mamma's awful sick, could Mr. Coburn come in and see her?"

It didn't take me long to get to the bedside of the sick woman. She was a distressing sight. Wild with pain, she was flinging herself about the bed and crying out, often with piercing screams. I found that the pain was in her stomach. Two or three neighbour women were present.

"How long has this been going on?" I asked.

"She took sick about noon," one of them answered. "She wasn't this bad at first. She has been getting worse all afternoon."

"Of course you've sent for the doctor?"

The women looked at one another and then one of them ventured: "N-no, Mr. Joyce is away and we didn't like to do it without his consent."

I nearly exploded. It was maddening to meet such stupidity. "You mean to tell me that you have let this woman suffer for five hours and made no effort to get a doctor? Well I'll soon fix that. Pray God it may not be too late."

The Joyce's had several horses. So I got hold of the oldest boy and said: "Now you hitch up your fastest horse, and start for town. Don't spare him. If he drops down dead when you get there it doesn't matter. If your mother doesn't get help she'll die. Now move fast."

The lad, thoroughly frightened, did as I had bidden him and he was soon away. As I returned to the house, I calculated that if the doctor was at home when the boy arrived and started immediately, it would be at least five hours or five and a half before he could arrive. Another look at the patient convinced me that if something was not done for her long before that he would be too late. I asked the women what they had done for her. They showed me a bottle of aconite and stated that they had given her several doses of it. I didn't know the nature of aconite, but had an idea it was a rather powerful poison. What could I do for her, that was the question. The only thing I could think of was a mixture which mother had often used at home and of which she had furnished me with a supply. She used it for a liniment and in case of cold or chills, would put a few drops in a cup of hot water for a drink. It was pretty hot stuff—cayenne pepper, camphor gum, whole cloves dissolved in alcohol. I knew the mixture in itself was harmless but I was afraid of what it might do on top of all that aconite. If the aconite was lying inactive in the woman's stomach, and then I gave her this dose and it started the drug to work it might kill her. What was I to do? Every moment I became more and more convinced that she would be beyond help if not dead when the doctor arrived.

I went into the parsonage and told my wife the predicament. We decided that there was nothing to be done but take the risk. If the sick woman's husband had been at home I would have explained the situation to him and allowed him to take the responsibility. I believe it was providential that he was away. He was a very cautious soul and I am almost sure would have decided to wait for the doctor. So I took my little bottle into the Joyce home, put nearly a quarter of a teaspoonful in a cup (I knew no ordinary dose would be of any use), filled the cup with hot water, put a little cream in it and took it to the sick woman. I did it with a most earnest prayer that the Great Healer would use it for her recovery. Mrs. Joyce seized the cup in both hands and drank the contents rapidly. How she could do so I do not know. It was very hot. Then I waited. Soon great belches of gas came from her, a few minutes later she threw up both hands and fairly shouted: "Mr. Coburn, oh thank God, the pain is all gone, every bit of it."

That alarmed me, I was afraid Mr. Aconite was getting in his deadly work, and that the sudden cessation of pain was simply the paralyzing of the nerves of the stomach. What might happen to the other nerves, I didn't know. I feared the worst.

Just before relief came Mr. Joyce returned. He sat down on the edge of the bed, placing his arm around his wife and resting her head on his shoulder. For a long time she would not let him move for fear a change of position might bring back the pain. Poor man, he was in a very uncomfortable position. It must have been a trying experience for him.

About ten-thirty the doctor arrived. It was a pitch dark night with pouring rain. He had on two overcoats and both were wet through. The roads there were so rough one could not have a cover on his buggy. It would shake it to pieces. One just had to take whatever weather he found.

The doctor was a rough and ready sort, a country doctor of the old school. He examined the patient and heard the story of the patient's suffering. Mrs. Joyce then told him that I had given her a drink of something that was awful hot, and that the pain left her very soon.

The old doctor looked at me and motioned for me to follow him into the kitchen: "What the deuce did you do to her?" he demanded.

I told him of my arrival about five o'clock and about what I found. I explained that after I had sent the boy for him I became convinced that if something was not done for her before he arrived it would be all up with her.

"And you were dead right about that my boy. I had a case like hers in every way, the other day. The woman was still alive when I arrived, but was past help and died soon after. But what did you do?" he persisted.

I told him about the aconite and my fears and then my decision to take the risk.

"What was in the mixture?" I told him.

"Well, if that doesn't beat the Dutch! Young man, I'll tell you this. If you had a degree from the finest medical school on the continent, you couldn't have given her anything more helpful. If I had been on the spot myself I couldn't have done better. No doubt at all you've saved the woman's life."

If I had only been quick enough in my thinking I would have asked the doctor to say nothing about it. Before I had time to think, the worthy doctor had informed the family and neighbour women as to the facts. To my great consternation my reputation as a doctor in the community went up several degrees.

While Muskoka is still a rough country and some of its roads none too smooth, conditions are vastly improved.

First the rural telephone cuts the time required to get a doctor in half. Then, the automobile can make the trip in far less time than the old horse and buggy. In case of need, a doctor can now be had in an hour or less.

3. *Two Brothers and a Plug of Tobacco*

On this mission field in Muskoka, one of my preaching places was a little log church. The soil was poor and as a consequence the people were poor also. I often wondered why, with such a wealth of fine productive soil in various parts of Canada to choose from, settlers chose such places as this. The only explanation I could find was that the land was at one time well timbered, and for many years the settlers obtained most of their income from the sale of the timber. But at the time now spoken of, the best timber had all been sold. It was only by the hardest work that people could wrest a living from the soil.

The majority of the early settlers here were Methodists. A little Methodist class had been organized by one of the "saddle-bag" preachers. Then the little group decided to build a church. Logs were freely donated. The members and adherents made "bees," felled the trees, cut them into the proper lengths and hewed them to make a flat surface on the inside, then free labour put them in place. A little cash was needed for doors, windows, flooring, seats, pulpit, etc. The church when finished would hold less than one hundred people. When I arrived, there were twelve members on the church roll. Of these, two brothers, John and Robert Elliott and their wives, constituted a third. The Elliott brothers were Irishmen, and because they said I was the only Irish "praicher" they had had for many years, they soon became staunch friends of mine. These men were poor. They lived on adjoining farms consisting of rough stony soil. Neither could afford a team of horses nor a full set of farm implements. So each had one horse, and they had their implements on shares. When necessary, they put the two horses together in a team and practically worked the two farms together. They were, in fact, dependent on each other for everything.

One autumn it was decided to hold a series of evangelistic services, or "protracted meetings," to use old Methodist phraseology. After a few nights I noticed that neither brothers nor their wives had been present. Now, when you have only twelve members, the absence of four of them cannot well go unnoticed. So one morning, I drove over to Robert's house to find out whether sickness or some other cause had kept them at home. Robert welcomed me quite heartily, but I sensed something peculiar in his manner and that of his wife.

"Are you all well, Robert?"

"Yes, sir, as well as usual, thank God."

"Well, Robert, none of your family have been over to the meetings."

"That's true, we haven't been out."

"But Robert, you were one of those most eager to have these meetings and you know there are so few of us. We need you. Why, may I ask, have you stayed at home? Surely you have some good reason. The folks down at the church can't make it out."

"I'd rather not give any reason. I will say this though, that it is nothing at all we have against the church nor you, Mr. Coburn."

"But Robert, that will not do. You were one of those who urged me to hold these meetings and now you don't support them. Come on now, as your minister and your friend, I have a right to know what is the trouble."

"Well then, I will say this: there is them that goes there, that my being there might not help, and I wouldn't want to stand in their way of gettin' good for they need it bad enough."

I was a little perplexed as to what he was driving at but

finally I said: "Do you mean, Robert, that you have had a quarrel with someone?"

"Well you can call it that if you like."

"Whom have you quarrelled with?"

"No sir, I don't wish to tell you that."

"But Robert, I must know. I cannot have a thing like this in my church without doing something about it. Is it Mr. So and so?"

"No sir."

"Is it so and so?"

"No sir."

One after the other I named off his neighbours within a radius of two or three miles. It was not any of them. Then all at once I remembered that John and his wife had been absent too. So I said: "Robert, it cannot be your own brother, John?"

"I made up my mind I would tell no one, but when you as our minister ask me a straight question, I can tell you no lie. It is. You are the only person outside the family that knows."

On visiting John's home I found the same situation. Both were quite sure that the other needed to "get good" at the meetings, and each was staying away so as not to interfere with the good work. From each of the men I got, almost verbatim, the same account of the quarrel.

Prior to my arrival on that circuit, the church shed at this place had fallen down. I called a meeting of the men and insisted on its being put in proper condition, so that on cold winter Sundays the horses would not suffer while the people worshipped the Lord in a comfortable church. A bee was organized. The first day a goodly number turned out. On succeeding days, however, the numbers dwindled until on the last day, only three men were left, the two Elliotts and an old man named Jensen. Jensen was in even poorer circumstances than were the Elliotts. On the afternoon of the last day when the job was almost finished,

Jensen said: "Well boys, I am out of tobacco. I will go over to the store and get me a plug."

"And say Jensen," said John Elliott, "when you are getting one for yourself you had better get one for me. You remember that plug you borrowed from me two or three years ago."

"All right," said Jensen.

When Jensen got out of hearing Robert said to John: "John Elliott, Jensen paid you that plug back."

"He did not."

"I say he did."

"I say he did not."

The argument grew fast and furious until Jensen hove in sight, then it ceased. Jensen handed a plug to John. John looked at him and asked if he had one for himself. Jensen rather sheepishly admitted that he had only ten cents and so could buy but one plug. At that John took his knife, cut the plug in two and gave Jensen half. (Afterwards Robert cited this as proof positive of John's guilt. He argued that John would never have given Jensen that half plug if his conscience hadn't condemned him.) Nothing more was said until the day's work was done. The Elliotts had about two miles to walk home. On the way the dispute again broke out. They finally stood at John's gate putting in the finishing touches to the argument. As a parting shot Robert said: "And there is something else, John Elliott, when our little church was built, you were the treasurer and no one knows to this day where all the money went."

That was too much for John. He raised his right hand (which many of the old country folk regarded as the sign of an oath) and solemnly declared: "Robert Elliott, until you take that back, I will never speak to you or have anything to do with you or anyone belonging to you, nor will I allow any belonging to me to do the same."

So here were these two men, their wives and children dependent on each other for so many things, each on his

own side of the fence, suffering acutely and yet too proud
to yield or to let anyone in the community know. The wives
were forbidden to speak. The children were not allowed
to play with each other. The men worked away, each on
his own farm, as best he could without the help of the
other. They were very much attached to each other and
they needed each other every day of their lives. If a child
in either home took sick, word was sent to the woman in the
other house who brought over any home remedies that she
thought might help. It was a very serious and unhappy
situation for them all.

At first I confess I found it hard to keep from a burst
of laughter. The fact that two middle aged men with
whiskers, fathers of children, would make such a fuss over
a plug of tobacco seemed almost absurd. My job, however,
as their minister was to try to heal the breach. But how?
I knew I had two stubborn, hot tempered blatherskites to
deal with. I was sure that if I brought them together and
let them talk, things would be said that would only make
matters worse. I spent two or three days going back and
forth from one house to the other. I adopted the plan of
dealing with each man separately, paring him down as it
were as much as he would stand at a sitting. Finally I
succeeded in persuading them each to agree to the same
formula. Part of the agreement was that they were to meet
each other in my presence, neither of them was to say one
word about the matter. I was to recite the terms of the
settlement. They were to shake hands and after that, they
were never to mention the affair either to each other or anyone else in the world.

I said to John: "John, you are the oldest. You had better
meet me at Robert's house tomorrow at 1.30 p.m."

"All right, Mr. Coburn, I'll be there."

So he was. Robert was in the woodshed when we
arrived. I said that we could have our little meeting out
here as well as anywhere else. Robert spoke up: "Mr.

Coburn, before you begin, will you just let me say one word."

"No Robert, not a word, not half a word. If I let you say your word, John will have a right to say a word too. Before we know where we are, you will be at it again as bad as ever. You know the agreement is that I am to recite the terms and you both are to say nothing. So, Robert, I will do the talking today if you please."

I then recited the terms, "John do you agree to that?"

"Yes sir."

"Robert, do you?"

"Yes sir."

"Shake hands, men," I said.

They stood and looked at each other but didn't move. I spoke again with considerable emphasis: "Shake hands." They obeyed. "Now then, down on your knees both of you." They both knelt in the chips and I prayed. I told the Lord how foolish and childish and stubborn and bad-tempered they both had been, how greatly they were ashamed of their conduct. I prayed that good common sense and the Grace of God might be given them in such measure that they would never sin in this way again. I knew that if I said these things directly to them they would probably get very angry and I would have another row on my hands. But they could not very well take offence at a prayer, and all that I said in the prayer was true and needed to be said.

In spite of the terms never to mention the matter to anyone in the world, each of these men confided in me that he had given in more than he really ought to have done but that he did it for my sake and that of the church.

The results were very happy. The men and their wives and children seemed almost like people released from prison. Two or three children in each home had not been baptized. They decided to have them all baptized at once. As Robert's house was the larger the baptismal party was held there. John and his wife brought their children to Robert's home and my wife and I were also invited. After the baptismal ceremony, a bountiful supper was served. After that I noticed that the tobacco was passed without the flicker of an eyelid.

4. *Should a Parson Play Checkers?*

I was finishing my third year on a country circuit of three appointments. The work on this field had been difficult. My predecessor, a very sincere and godly man, had been utterly lacking in tact. He was afflicted with what might well be called Enlargement of the Conscience, that often got him and others into trouble. He had succeeded in having a glorious row at each of the appointments. So unpleasant had the situation become that the Stationing Committee deemed it wise to remove him at the close of his second year. Most of the people were so much relieved at his departure that they rallied to my support with great enthusiasm. The field had been a mission but now asserted its independence. Two beautiful churches had been built and in each case the cost had been met by cash or *bona fide* subscriptions. The membership of the churches had also substantially increased.

Until that time it had been the invariable rule of the Methodist Church that a minister could not remain longer than three years on any circuit. The last General Conference, however, had amended the rule making it possible for one to remain a fourth or even a fifth year, provided he received an invitation from the Quarterly Board supported by a three-fourths vote of its members, and if such invitation was endorsed by a two-thirds vote of the all powerful Stationing Committee.

At a regular meeting of the Board, one of the members in a short speech recited some of these facts, called attention to the change in the Church's law and moved that the preacher be invited to remain another year. The motion was seconded. In such cases it was the duty of the Recording Steward (the chief lay official) to put the motion. Old John Murchison occupied that position. He was a man with very little education. A very moderate dose of the three R's was all he had received. He was notoriously close in money matters, narrow in his views and desperately stubborn. He now stood up and instead of putting the motion, delivered himself as follows:

"Well men, I don't deny that what you have said about our preacher is true, but I think for one thing it's time for him to move on. Three years has been the rule in the Methodist Church, and it has worked well. No minister has ever stayed longer than three years on this circuit. I don't hold with these new fangled ideas."

That speech made quite a stir. Some of the men were quite indignant. One, more persistent than the rest, expressed the opinion that there was something behind all this.

"Come Murchison," he said, "be a man and if you have anything against Mr. Coburn, out with it."

"Yes," said another, "that's right. The fact that he has been here three years is no good reason why he shouldn't stay a fourth. You'll have to do better than that, John."

At last old John got to his feet again:

"Well, to tell the truth," he said, "I don't like to have things dished up to me about our preacher."

"What's been dished up and who's been doing the dishing, John?"

Then one of the most level-headed of the group addressed John:

"Now John, you've either said too much or too little. You have no right to make vague charges like that. We are all Mr. Coburn's friends and we won't stand for it. Now either take back what you have said or tell us exactly what you mean."

"Hear, hear," came from all sides. Poor old John, he was greatly embarrassed and confused. He hadn't counted on getting into such a box when he began.

"Well," he said, "I didn't mean to raise all this fuss, but I don't like to hear our preacher criticized an' I think that a preacher of the Gospel should have nothin' to do with worldly and sinful things an' it has been dished up to me several times that Mr. Coburn plays checkers."

Several of the men burst into hearty laughter.

"Is that all?" they asked him.

"Yes, that's all I have to say."

When the laughter had subsided one of the men said:

"John Murchison, I'm surprised at you. I did give you credit for some common sense. You ought to be ashamed of yourself. I raised three sons, as you know. Many's the evening in our own home I played checkers and other games with them. I taught them to play. Wasn't that better than having them go out God knows where to find their amusement? If in his own home or in theirs Mr. Coburn plays a game with the boys maybe he will do them as much good that way as by a sermon. I only hope he plays a good game. Say, Coburn, the first time you visit my home we'll have a go at it, eh? Now, John, no more nonsense. You put that motion and let us get on with business."

Very reluctantly John complied. He was accustomed to have his own way on that Board, but every hand but his own was raised in support. He did not vote against it and he was compelled to record a unanimous vote. I thanked the brethren for their loyalty and confidence and said that while we did not share Brother Murchison's opinions he had a perfect right to express them. In fact I respected him for having had the courage to say what he had to my face rather than behind my back.

6

THE CHURCH AT TERRA NOVA

EARLY in my ministry I had charge of a rural field of which Terra Nova appointment was one of three. The land around Terra Nova was rough and hilly, the soil light and stony. Only by hard, hard work and thrift could any family attain a comfortable standard of living. None were rich. A few enjoyed moderate comfort, but the majority were poor and found it a constant problem to make ends meet.

For years the congregation had worshipped in a building most unsuitable for such a purpose. It was unsightly in appearance, being made of rough lumber and never having had any paint. It was far too small for the congregation. Its ceiling was very low and on a hot summer's day the heat almost unbearable in the crowded place. It certainly did not tend to produce a spirit of worship, and the hour of service in this place was 2.30 p.m., when the day was hottest. The seats were hard, uncomfortable, wooden benches. As a matter of fact the building had not been built for a church in the first place, but as a hall in which meetings could be held. Years before there had been two small congregations, one about two miles to the south and the other an equal distance to the north of Terra Nova. It was decided to amalgamate these two congregations. It was perfectly natural for them to hold their meetings in this hall. The arrangement when made was intended to be only temporary. But time went on, money was none too plentiful and so nothing had been done to secure a more suitable place of worship.

A fine new church had been built at Honeywood, another appointment on the same circuit, and, contrary to the prophecies of some timid souls, its cost had been completely covered by the subscriptions of the people. At the opening service of the Honeywood Church one of the progressive young men from Terra Nova came to me and said:

"Mr. Coburn, we need a new church at Terra Nova, just as badly, perhaps more so, than they needed one here. That old shack is not fit for use as a place of worship. Won't you come down and help us build one?"

I agreed with the young man though I saw difficulties. The people of Honeywood were quite able to build and pay for their church. Many were well off. Terra Nova was different. To add to the difficulty, the congregation was, for a country place, fairly large. The problem was to build a church large enough for the congregation and yet within the very limited resources of the people. That was a difficult problem but it was solved.

I called a meeting of the members and adherents of the church. All were agreed, young and old, that a new church was needed; the old building could not be repaired and enlarged. But the majority of the older men were afraid of the cost. They dreaded having a debt that might burden them for years. The young people on the other hand were all for going ahead. In some cases a father was on one side of the argument and a son on the other. The young people had the support of two of the older men, one of whom was the father of a large family. These people being nearly all of Irish descent, a good lively argument ensued but all in the very finest spirit and temper. After every angle of the situation had been thoroughly probed and discussed the vote was taken and the progressives won by a small margin.

At first the opponents of building (if you could call them such) were inclined to hold back and take no part in the enterprise. That would have been fatal. The task was so great and their resources were so meagre that only if everyone did his part could they hope for success. These men and women, however, were sincere and devout. They loved their church. Finally all came heartily into line and the work proceeded. Some of the hardest work and the most sacrificial giving came from those who had at first opposed the plan.

I was able to interest some wealthy people in Toronto who donated a few hundreds of dollars, but the people of Terra Nova themselves bore by far the larger part of the burden. The men worked for days, digging the cellar for the basement and (with their teams) hauling the materials. Then out of their slender means they gave money with a liberality I have never seen equalled. What sacrifices it involved none but God and themselves could ever know. As a result a beautiful church was built and the cost provided in cash and subscriptions that were nearly all paid in full. It was of frame construction with brick veneer. As lumber was plentiful and comparatively cheap, we could get more church for our money that way than any other. The basement was fitted up for a Sunday School hall and for the holding of week night meetings. The auditorium was bright, being well lighted with eight windows, four on each side in Romanesque style. They had white panes in the centre and soft quiet tones of stained glass in the margins. The walls and ceiling were lathed and plastered in pure white. There was an alcove for the choir behind the pulpit. The pews were modern and very comfortable. The people were proud of their little church and with good reason. Without extravagance or gaudiness it had simple beauty. It was a place of worship.

One splendid instance of their sacrificial giving came to my knowledge. There was an Irish family named Campbell who lived on one of those rough stony farms. They had done more than their share in both work and cash. The day the church was dedicated old Robert approached me: "How much more do we need, Misther Coburn, to pay for the church?"

"Oh, I think five or six hundred dollars will square everything up pretty well."

"And how much of that do you think is our share?"

"Robert," I said, "you and your family have worked so hard and given so much already, I just can't lay any further burden on you."

"It's rale nice to hear you say that sorr, though I don't think we've done any more than we ought to a done. But I'll let you into a little secret. Maybe you have noticed that the coat mother wears is getting a bit shabby and thin. Me and the children planned to get her a new coat for Christmas. We were goin' to thry hard and get her a fur coat or a fur-lined one, that would keep her poor ould bones warm the rest of her life. It was all a dead secret, but she was too sharp for us. Whether I talk in my sleep or what, I don't know. But the other morning after breakfast she says: 'Wait Robert, before you and Will go out to the barn I want to talk to yez. I've found out about the new coat yez are plannin' to give me. An' I could do well with a new coat. It would be fine on cold days. But Robert, I've figgered it all out. You can't buy that coat and give what is needed to the church. There must be no debt on the House of God. So Robert, I want you to give what is needed to the church and I'll make the ould coat do another winther.'

So that's how it is sorr, and if ye plaze will ye tell me how much our share of the balance will be?"

The work we had done together created a strong bond between that congregation and me. After I had gone to other fields I was from time to time invited to return and preach on anniversary and other occasions. So I went up to preach and join in celebrating the thirty-second anniversary of the dedication of the church. The services were to be in the afternoon and evening. I had preached in the morning at Hornings Mills, nine miles away. The minister, his wife and I were at dinner when the 'phone rang. "Terra Nova Church is on fire," was the message.

We learned afterwards that a spark from the chimney had ignited the roof. We hurried out and found the beautiful building a pile of smoking ruins. There was no water system, and no ladder long enough to reach the roof. The neighbours had quickly assembled in response to a general telephone alarm, and had succeeded in getting the pews and other furniture safely out.

The burning of Terra Nova's little church was a heart-rending tragedy. It was the only church of any kind within a radius of several miles and was the social as well as the religious centre of that community. The basement was used for meetings of various kinds. As I looked at the ruins I thought of all the sacrifice and hard work that had gone into that building. No one else could know that as well as I.

The members of the Board of Trustees who had worked with me were all dead but one, a little man, Hercules Ritchie, now a feeble old man of 84. He was one of the most sincere and devoted Christians I ever knew. I found him and his good wife silently weeping. Outside their family they had few interests except in that church. It was everything to them. I comforted them as best I could and then turned to face a company of two hundred stricken people. Some were in their Sunday best, others in working clothes with smudges of smoke and ashes on hands and face. The minister, an elderly man, Mr. Young, seemed to be completely upset, confused and helpless.

Then a strange thing happened. It seemed as if the thirty-two years had vanished, and I was back among them again as their minister and leader. Without fully realizing what I was doing, I just took charge of the situation. I felt they must not be allowed to disperse without a service.

It was a lovely warm day in October—one of those charming days that our stern Canadian climate often gives us at that time of year. So the organ, pulpit and pews were arranged in order. But what was I to preach about? The sermon I had prepared for the anniversary celebration would not do at all. Then I remembered that at the dedication thirty-two years before I had preached at one of the services. I could not recall one word of the sermon—a good thing, no doubt. I did, however, recall the text: "On this rock will I build my church and the gates of hell shall not prevail against it." *The indestructibility of the Church.* That was the word for this hour. We opened the service with Cowper's great hymn: "God moves in a mysterious way His wonders to perform."

We read that wonderful little poem that has been the comfort and inspiration of God's people in times of dire distress, the forty-sixth Psalm:

"God is our refuge and strength, a very present help in trouble. Therefore will not we fear, though the earth be removed and though the mountains be carried into the midst of the sea.

"There is a river, the streams whereof shall make glad the City of God, the holy place of the tabernacles of the most High.

"God is in the midst of her; she shall not be moved. God shall help her and that right early.

"The Lord of Hosts is with us; the God of Jacob is our refuge."

After prayer we sang again: "Oh God of Bethel by whose hand thy people still are fed."

Then I preached. I had no time to prepare, but I can honestly say I never preached with greater ease and freedom, and without boasting, I think I ought to add, with power too. The ideas seemed to pour into my mind and the words came without any difficulty. The burden of my message was that the real church was indestructible, that it did not consist of wood and stone, but of men and women in whose hearts there dwelt the faith and love of God. No fire can burn that.

"This beautiful building that we all loved so much is burned, but the church in Terra Nova is not destroyed, it is here in your hearts and I am sure that the same devotion that your fathers and mothers showed thirty-two years ago will be shown by you, their children, and that you will see that the church has a suitable building." Then we sang: "I love Thy Kingdom Lord, the house of Thine abode."

It is not often given to a preacher to see immediate tangible results of a sermon but I surely did so on this occasion. Announcement was made that the following evening a meeting would be held in the home of one of the members to make plans for a new church. Good old Hercules Ritchie hobbled up to me, leaning on his cane, reached out his hand and said: "Coburn, all isn't lost is it?" The tears had gone and there was the light of joy and victory in his old eyes. The whole congregation seemed imbued with the same spirit.

When the church was built I had placed an insurance policy for its full value, but since then costs of building had trebled. The good people had faithfully paid the premiums but had not thought of increasing the amount. The insurance was therefore quite inadequate. The fire occurred at the very depth of the depression, when prices of farm produce were very low. Potatoes sold for fifteen cents a bag. I was able to interest two wealthy friends in Toronto who gave me about seven hundred and fifty dollars for the cause. The people took that, and the insurance money and, as their fathers had done before, out of meagre resources gave enough to build another church just as attractive and commodious, in fact almost a replica of the one destroyed.

They insisted that I should go back and dedicate the new building. Again I found an appropriate text: "And the glory of this latter house shall be greater than that of the former."

7

BOUTS WITH JOHN BARLEYCORN

1. *The Battle of Forty Bars*

In 1908 a strong agitation arose in Toronto for a reduction in the number of bar-rooms. There were 150 hotels with bar-room licenses. This was far in excess of the needs of the city for hotel accommodation. Many of these places furnished practically no accommodation to the travelling public, but were mainly drinking dens, often resorted to by criminals and confirmed drunkards. According to the liquor law then in force in Ontario, the Council of any municipality could, by by-law, limit the number of taverns or bar-room licenses to be issued by the license commissioners within its bounds. In response to urgent appeals by citizens—not all of them total abstainers—the City Council arranged to take a plebiscite on the regular municipal election day, the first Monday in January, 1909, as to whether 40 bar-rooms should be closed, leaving the number at 110. It is safe to say that never in the history of the city up to that time, had the "wet" and "dry" forces been so thoroughly organized as for this battle.

I was at the time the Minister of Parliament Street Methodist Church, situated in Ward 2. Ward 2 was one of the wettest wards in the city. It had three breweries and a large number of taverns. The Ward Committee insisted on my being the ward organizer. At first I refused, urging that my church work would not permit it. Finally, however, I agreed to leave the decision to my church board. The Committee met the Board on a Sunday morning after service. They made a strong plea and I stated my position:

"Please understand that this has come to me like a bolt from the blue. You all know how glad I would be to do anything in the fight against booze, but I can't see how I can do this. My hands are more than full of church work as you all well know. For the next six weeks this organizing is a full time job. If you grant the committee's request you must release me from practically all church work. Oh, I have some old sermons in the proverbial preacher's barrel that with little effort I could fix up to preach to you. But if I take this job, I cannot be responsible for any pastoral or other detailed work of the church. Now it's up to you. If you consent, I can hardly refuse, but you must do so with your eyes open and remember if the church should suffer, you will be responsible, not I."

One of the committee here interposed with a statement that they would gladly pay for any assistance that might be needed to care for my work. Then, Arthur Corscadden, the Recording Steward, one of the finest Christian men I ever knew spoke:

"Mr. Chairman, I think this church has been highly honoured this morning, and has been offered a magnificent opportunity to render service for the Kingdom of God. I quite understand our pastor's hesitation and his fear that the Church might suffer. I would remind him, that he has preached to us that we should have faith in God, that we should give ourselves in service to humanity and that if we do God's will we need not fear consequences. That applies to the church as well as to individuals. This seems to me a clear call of duty. Let's put some of Mr. Coburn's preaching into practice."

There were "hear, hears" and fervent "amens" from all sides. Corscadden continued:

"I am glad to see that you agree with me. I then move, that this Board consent to this proposition and release our pastor from the work of the church until voting day, and that a committee be appointed to arrange for the carrying on of his work. Of course we hope Mr. Coburn will preach to us as often as he can. Those old sermons will be new to us."

The motion was seconded, put and to my astonishment unanimously and enthusiastically carried.

Next day I plunged into the new job. The first task was the revision of the voters' list. That list is made up from the assessment roll, compiled in April or May. It was now November. During the intervening months many people had changed residence. Some had lost their right to vote in the ward, while others had acquired that right. A thorough canvass must therefore be made. The revision of the voters' list in Toronto had been carried on very loosely. Candidates for the Council could prepare a list of their supporters, appeal to have them added to the list, go before the judge and by swearing they were entitled to vote, have their names placed on the list. Hearsay evidence was accepted. I had been at this task only a few days when I saw the possibilities of crookedness. I sent out a number of reliable men to hang around bar-rooms, drinking ginger ale and pop and listening to what might be said. One great disadvantage the "wets" always labour under, they nearly all drink and a drink or two has wonderful powers to unloose the tongue. My spies brought back reports that convinced me that the grand strategy of our opponents was to pad the voters' list with fraudulent names, then bring over a group of expert impersonators from Buffalo, who would go from poll to poll all day and vote.

When all appeals had been filed we found that while

the dry forces in the whole city had applied to add 1,800 names, our opponents had 3,800.

Next day seven stenographers were placed in the City Clerk's office. All the names were copied and then investigated. Some of them were names of dead people, others of little children, and hundreds were purely fictitious. Now, as the Court of Revision is not a Court of Record it would be difficult to prove who had given the evidence in any specific case. The enemy had counted on that. Their workers could go into the box and swear the names on with practically no fear of detection. His Honour, the late Judge Winchester, a very able jurist was the presiding judge. We went to him the day before court opened, letting him know what we had discovered and asking for protection. When court opened the Judge said:

"I am going to do something not usually done in this court. I am going to swear in a stenographer and have the evidence all taken down."

The lawyer for the wets made vigorous protest:

"Your Honour, this is going a little too far. The other day one of these temperance cranks (meaning myself) made a speech in which wild charges were made about the methods my clients were using. These people are always making wild statements. I did not think Your Honour would pay any attention to them."

"Mr. Curry," replied the Judge, "No one has so far made any charges in this Court. I have an unusually long list of appeals to hear this week. Some mistakes might be made."

Then he added significantly: "And it might be very desirable to be able to determine just who had made the mistakes. No one who is telling the truth can have any objection to recording the evidence. We will proceed."

It was a battle royal. Our opponents laboured under two difficulties. Several of their workers could not abstain, and were at times in a somewhat befuddled state. Then they had their lists mixed, and in some cases could not be sure which were *bona fide* and which were bogus. With a stenographer recording every word, it was a risky business to go into the box and swear to doubtful statements. A penitentiary cell might be the outcome.

While the court was dealing with the appeals from Ward 2, one of the leaders on the other side approached me:

"Say, Coburn, can't we come to some arrangement about this?"

"Certainly," I replied, "I have no desire to deprive anyone of a vote to which he is entitled. I know all about your list, and am willing that all so entitled be placed on the voters' list."

We two then made out a list of names. It was handed up to the Judge.

"What is this?" he said.

One of the lawyers explained that we had agreed to have these names added.

The Judge looked down at me and said: "Mr. Coburn, is that correct?"

"Yes, Your Honour, if you wish I can furnish the evidence here and now to put these names on. I can also furnish evidence showing that the other names presented by our opponents should not go on. I understand that they will withdraw these latter names."

This was agreed to by both sides and made effective by the Judge.

Following Ward 2 came Ward 3. My colleague, the organizer for 3 did not have his work in as good shape as we had in Ward 2. That was not his fault but owing to lack of workers.

Fortunately our opponents were not aware of the situation. To our great amusement and delight, when Ward 3 was called, the opposing counsel rose and said:

"To save the time of the court, we wish to withdraw some of these names."

He read for over an hour withdrawing over 400 names.

When the five day court battle was over, out of the 3,800 appeals, our opponents succeeded in placing on the list only 1,300. We won at the polls by only 846 votes. Obviously that fight was won at the Court of Revision.

The story of the battle in that Court furnished headlines for Toronto newspapers for a week and had three results:

1. Experienced municipal politicians declared that it was probably the cleanest election ever held in Toronto.

2. Forty low dives were closed.

3. The slipshod method of revising the voters' list was abolished. Ever since that time all applications for additions to the list are investigated by a civic official.

Incidentally one of our opponents paid me what I have regarded as one of the finest compliments I have ever received. One night in the court room, he came up to me reaching out his hand and said: "Shake, Coburn. I'll say this for you, you fight damned hard, but you fight damned fair."

2. *Tommy Monteith—His Victory*

Early in my ministry I was holding a series of revival services. In the village there lived a man in his late thirties. He was a tailor. He was one of the friendliest, most jovial souls one could meet. Everybody liked Tommy when he was sober. His one great weakness was drink. His mother had died when he was quite young. His father was a genuine old Scotch Presbyterian, but I fancy had little tact in managing a growing boy. Tommy and his father, who was the village postmaster, lived with a widowed sister of Tommy's who kept house. Tommy had a few friends who like himself were fond of the drink. As there was no bar room within twelve miles, they used to bring their liquor to Tommy's tailor shop. Often the sleep of the neighbours was disturbed by the sounds of revelry by night that issued from that place.

One Saturday morning as I was busy preparing my work

for Sunday I got thinking of Tommy and could not banish him from my mind. Again and again I asked myself, "Why not go over and see what can be done with Tommy? No one in this community needs religion more than he." The mail came each day by stage (a horse drawn vehicle) at 3 p.m. When I had received my mail I went into Tommy's shop, next door to the post office. For a wonder, Tommy was perfectly sober, sitting on his bench making a pair of pants. He greeted me in his usual friendly way. We cracked a few jokes and talked for a little about things in general. Finally I went over and looking him straight in the face said, "Tommy, don't you think it is high time you made a change in your way of life? You are too good a chap to waste your life in the way that you and I know you are doing. I am here to tell you of One who is able and willing to help you if you are ready to do your part."

Tommy just looked at me for a minute or two without speaking and then burst out, "Well I'll be gol darned. That's the third crack I've had on that subject inside half an hour."

"How's that, what do you mean Tommy?"

"Well first I got a letter from my girl in Toronto today. You know she's a regular peach. She and I have been sweet on each other for ten years. She's a real true blue Christian and she won't marry me because I drink, although she says I'm the only fellow in the world for her."

"Well Tommy, your girl is evidently not only a good girl but a wise one. No woman should put her happiness in the care of a man who drinks as you do."

"Yes, I guess that's so. Well, she wrote me a letter about becoming a Christian myself. Then my old Dad wrote me a letter on the same subject and put it in my mail. I had just finished reading these two letters when in you come and get after me on the same tack—something funny about it I'm thinking."

"No Tommy, nothing funny at all. Evidently the Spirit

of God is seeking you. He is here and in Toronto too. He, no doubt, has put it in the hearts of your sweetheart and your father to write their letters. All morning something has seemed to urge me to come and see you."

I could see that Tommy was serious and deeply impressed. I went over to the window and pulled down the blind. Then I locked the door.

"What are you going to do?" said Tommy in some surprise.

"You and I are going to have a little conversation with the Lord about this and I don't want any interruptions. So get down here with me."

"Oh Mr. Coburn, I couldn't pray. I really couldn't."

"Never mind, I'll do the praying, at least out loud. You can follow silently if you will. Come on now Tommy."

Tommy obeyed.

My prayer was not a long one but was to the point. I told the Lord about Tommy and how he needed Divine help, also about the fine little girl in Toronto, and prayed that her prayers as well as those of Tommy's father might be answered. A very sober and subdued Tommy arose from his knees. Then I asked him to promise to come to the church the following Sunday evening. He very readily agreed. I went home, but on thinking the whole thing over I remembered that Sunday was often the very worst day for Tommy and his gang. Being off work and having nothing else to do they usually got drunk. I knew Tommy was quite sincere in promising to come to church but there was every likelihood that long before church time he would be so drunk that it would never occur to him.

That winter the snow was deep and the roads bad. I was not feeling too well. The doctor had told me that to drive my horse around the circuit and preach three times was too much for me and that I ought to get someone to drive me. I had been told that Tommy was very fond of a horse.

These two facts suggested a plan of action. After supper I went back to Tommy's shop.

"What are you doing tomorrow Tommy?" I said.

"Nothing particular, why, what's on your mind?"

"How would you like to go for a drive?"

"That sounds good. Nothing I like better than a ride behind a good horse."

"Well Tommy, my horse is no prize winner but she's all I have. You know I've been going a pretty lively pace and I'm pretty tired. The doctor says I oughtn't to preach three times on Sunday and drive the horse all round the field. I would be very glad and grateful to you if you will come with me and drive. How about it?"

"Sure thing. I'll be glad to go. What time do you want to start?"

I felt sure it would work because when sober, Tommy was the most good natured of chaps. He would do anything to oblige anyone. So it was settled. Tommy went with me. In my preaching that day I had only one person in mind. The people at the afternoon appointment were most friendly and often urged me to stay at one of their houses for supper. I decided to stay on this occasion and arranged to start back home for the evening service just in time to put the horse away and get to the church at the proper hour. If any of the "gang" happened to be about I didn't want them to have the opportunity to get hold of Tommy to give him a drink.

Coming home we had to climb a long hill. The horse must be allowed to walk all the way. Conversation between us had died down. After a long silence, suddenly Tommy burst out with "Well if I'm not the gol darndest fool in the County of Dufferin!"

"Well well Tommy, when did you make that discovery?"

"Just now, here I've had just a bully day, never enjoyed myself better in my life and tomorrow morning I can look the whole world in the face. You know, Mr. Coburn, after

I've been out on a toot, I don't remember anything that's happened. I don't know who I've insulted or what mean things I've done or said, an' I'm scared to look at any person. Now ain't I a proper kind of fool?"

"Bully for you Tommy. That's the talk I wanted to hear. Now don't you think the time has come to change all that?"

"Oh, if I only could, but it's no use. I've been at it too long. You never drank. You don't know the hold that stuff gets on a fellow. I could never do it, not me."

"Tommy I can promise you this—if you really want to lead a new life you'll get all the help you need to do it."

"Say that again, will you?"

I repeated the statement.

"Are you sure that's true?"

"Why yes, Tommmy, I have it on the best of authority." I quoted some of the promises of the Bible. Then I told him of Jerry McCauley, the jail bird and river thief of New York who was far farther down than Tommy had ever dreamed of, and who was not only redeemed but was the means of saving hundreds like himself.

"You do your part Tommy and God will do his," I urged.

"Well, by golly, it won't do any harm to try."

"Then Tommy, strike while the iron's hot. Take the step tonight. At the close of my sermon tonight I will invite any who desire to accept Christ to come forward. Now you make the break. You'll never be sorry."

"I'll do it, Mr. Coburn. But remember I'm a pretty poor tool. You and the Lord will have to help me along considerable."

"Both of us will be right with you, don't fear Tommy."

When we arrived at the little church it was packed. Tommy got a seat just inside the door. It was easy to preach that night. When I gave the invitation, without a moment's hesitation, Tommy arose and came forward. If a bomb had burst in the midst of that congregation the people could hardly have been more surprised. I detected a distinct snicker and even some of the saints scarcely knew what to think. Some thought that Tommy was "tight" and had possibly done it in a dare or a bet. They soon found out, however, that Tommy was in dead earnest. At the close of the service he made a little speech which though clothed in very unconventional language left no doubt as to its sincerity. That night Tommy Monteith and drink parted forever. To the credit of the rough fellows comprising his gang, it must be said that not one of them made any effort to lure him back to their ways. More than one of them congratulated him on his stand and wished him the best of luck. Tommy joined the church. We made him an usher, a position he filled to everybody's satisfaction.

His girl kept him on probation for over two years. Then one day in the spring I went into his shop. He seized my hand and started a pump handle action, dancing around me, laughing and saying, "She'll have me, she'll have me."

At first I was alarmed and feared that Tommy had fallen off the water wagon but he soon put my fears at rest. "I've had a letter from Ruth. She's willing to marry me now. When do you go to Conference?"

I gave him the date.

"Well no one else but you will do this job. If I go down with you at Conference time, could you marry us in Toronto?"

"Certainly Tommy, and no wedding could give me greater pleasure."

Tommy brought home his bride. A fine, sensible, wholesome Christian girl she was. They decided to go West. The whole countryside turned out to give them a farewell and to present them with a substantial sum of money. Tommy got a job clerking in a store in one of the thriving towns of Saskatchewan. He homesteaded on a quarter section (160 acres) about 10 miles from town. He managed to get a small house and barn, as required by the homestead regulations, erected. For three years, he and his wife lived for six months in each year in the little house and Tommy "biked" to town and back each day. At the end of three years, having fulfilled his settlement duties, Tommy received his patent of the land. Shortly afterwards he sold it and with the money received made a down-payment on a house in town. There he and his wife established a home.

Many years later I visited this town and Tommy insisted that I should be his guest. There were three fine children. These youngsters knew nothing whatever of their father's old life. Tommy had set up a repair, cleaning and pressing establishment of his own. His unfailing courtesy and delightful sense of humour made him a favourite in the town. He showed me his books and they revealed that his business netted him an income of over two thousand dollars a year.

"If I hadn't changed my ways, I'd have been a long time getting that much money," he remarked to me.

Tommy lived until a little over seventy years of age. At his death he left three splendid children, all in good positions and enjoying the respect and confidence of the whole community. For his widow he was able to provide a comfortable home, free of debt, and a substantial amount in cash and life insurance. Shortly before his death he said to his wife: "Ruth dear, never let anyone tell you there is nothing in religion. I know there is. I've proved it and I'm satisfied that death won't be the finish either. Let it come— the sooner the better, I'm not afraid."

8

MORE BOUTS WITH JOHN BARLEYCORN

1. *An Irish Alcoholic*

ONE night about ten o'clock I was on my way home to the parsonage of old Parliament St. Methodist Church, Toronto. I fell in with a chap who asked me where he could get a drink. He was quite sober, but his breath made it plain that he had had a drink or two already. I told him I was not interested in helping fellows to get drinks, and asked him to forget about it and slip away home to bed.

"By the sound of your voice I think you must be Irish," he said. I pleaded guilty.

"So am I." With that he turned and walked with me.

"I'm a very lonely man. I've no friends or relatives here, so a talk with one of my own race for a little will make me feel better—if I'm not intruding sir."

"Not at all my friend, come along."

He told me he was an honour graduate of Dublin University, a chartered accountant, a trained musician, having played the pipe organ in some of Canada's large churches.

"But sir," said he, "that is all over and done with. You may as well know I'm down and out. The man you're walking this street with is just a drunken bum. For the past six weeks sir, I have slept on the straw behind the horses in one of the fire station stables. Oh, I know it's against the rules but I've nowhere else to go and the boys at that station are all Irish. They warned me that they mustn't find me there, but they leave a window open at night—for ventilation of course. I crawl in after ten p.m. and out again before six a.m."

After some hesitation he came with me into the parsonage, where everyone had gone to bed. When he saw the piano his face lit up and he asked if he might play a little.

"Go ahead," I said, "play anything you wish."

I wasn't prepared for what followed. He swept that keyboard with the hands of a master. The piano was a good one and recently tuned. Soon there came from it such music as I had never heard before in our home. My wife was upstairs preparing for bed. She wondered what in the world was going on. One thing she knew right well, that her husband wasn't making that music. So, reclothing herself she came down. In another room upstairs two young girls, friends of ours who were visiting us were in bed though not asleep. They too heard the music and wondered. They dressed and came down. We all sat entranced, as the musician, apparently oblivious of anybody's presence, continued. Then suddenly he stopped and said to me:

"Would it be all right if I sang a little?"

"Why sure, man, sing or anything else you like."

Then to a soft and lovely accompaniment, he sang that old, sweet, sad song of the Irish poet Thomas Moore, "The Last Rose of Summer." Of course my wife and the girls did not know the story, but to me it seemed that into that song the singer put all the anguish and frustration of his wasted life. When he finished, I whispered to my wife, "Please make us a bit of lunch. Make good strong coffee, as strong as anyone can possibly drink it."

We had a delightful time around the table. Our guest was a real Irishman, quick witted and genial. For the time the sadness was all forgotten. All at once, with a start, he said, "What time is it, Mr. Coburn?"

"A quarter past eleven."

"Oh, and isn't it the slick one ye are, ye knew well enough the bars all close at eleven. You were determined to cheat me out of a bit of a drink tonight, weren't ye?"

"You needn't worry," I said, "you won't have to go any further tonight. You'll stay with us."

"No, Mr. Coburn, I'm not fit to get into any decent bed. I haven't had my clothes off for six weeks."

"Oh well, if you feel that way about it, we'll make you a shakedown here on the floor. I'm not going to let you go back to that stable tonight."

My wife and the girls cleared off the table and then retired. When they had gone I said: "Harry, in God's name, how did a man like you come to this?"

"Well may you ask that question," he answered. "I had a good home and was well brought up. My parents gave me a good education. I had every chance. But I was a young fool. I knew what liquor had done to many, but I was sure it could not happen to me. A man with my education and with my background would never be caught that way. I could drink and let it alone, at any rate I would try it out."

"It didn't work out very well. Your experiment wasn't a success, was it?" I asked.

"I should say not," was the reply, "why is it that well educated people so often make fools of themselves? I ought to have known better, that no one can safely experiment on himself with alcohol. If I had only listened to the voice of science. It tells us that alcohol's immediate effect is on the brain cells. It slows their activity. So the mind is less active. One thing I completely overlooked, that alcohol is a habit forming drug. I was going to be a moderate drinker. I had no thought of anything else, but before I knew where I was the habit had me in its grip."

"Harry, I would like to ask you one question. Suppose you had your life to live over again—from your boyhood in your father's home, what would you do about drinking?"

"What would I do? Need you ask me that?" Grasping one of my knees in a grip that made me wince, he exclaimed in a voice choked with emotion:

"Oh sir, if I could only start over again. I'd never touch a drop of the infernal stuff. It's the devil's own brew. In my young days I thought the teetotallers, as we called them, were fanatics and fools. I know now that they were right. Alcohol is a narcotic poison. It's dangerous and it does no one any real good. Oh, I know a little will make a fellow feel gay and happy but only for a time. It makes no real contribution to one's life—and look at the price one may have to pay. Oh, my God, what a price I've paid and I'm only one of thousands. If you break a test tube in a laboratory you can get another for a few cents, but if you try some silly experiment with your life and ruin it you can't get another. That's what I did. I gambled Mr. Coburn and lost. I am truly and hopelessly lost."

"Oh, I wouldn't say that," I urged.

"But I do say it. I know it. Mr. Coburn you can have no idea what a hold this desire for drink has upon me. It is like a fire within me. I would do almost anything to get it. I have tried again and again to overcome the habit only to fall deeper and deeper. Now I think I know what's in your mind. Your bringing me into your home and keeping me until the bars had closed indicates that you want to help me. But I ask you, please do not try. Many others, ministers and kind hearted folk have tried hard—but all to no avail. Time and money have been spent only to be wasted. No, I've had my chance. No one is to blame but myself. I am no good to myself or anyone else nor ever will be—just let me go my way."

In spite of Harry's request, which I believe was quite sincere, I did try to help him. I used methods that had brought success in other cases. I did everything I could think of only to be met by complete failure. A short time after he disappeared. I could get no trace of him and never saw or heard of him again.

In late years when that strange but splendid organization known as "Alcoholics Anonymous" had come into existence, and by the use of its own peculiar methods has succeeded in restoring to normal manhood many who were regarded as hopeless victims of the drink habit, I have often thought of my Irish friend, Harry Johnston. Alcoholics Anonymous has often succeeded where all other methods have failed. They might have saved him, but the idea had not yet been born.

2. *A Devil Cast Out*

In modern times many sincere seekers after truth have found in the miracles of the Bible a real difficulty for faith. There is one miracle, however, that has given me no trouble at all—the casting of the devils out of the man of Gadara, and his restoration to sanity and wholesome living. I have seen that miracle enacted, in various forms, over and over again. One of these cases occurred in the little Methodist Church, Bethesda, at Crow's Corners in the Township of Sunnidale. Evangelistic services had been in progress for several weeks. Two earnest women of the church decided to visit the homes of all the people in the neighbourhood who did not go to church. One day they went to the home of a farmer Ab. Browne, who was a notorious drunkard. After some conversation they had prayer with Mrs. Browne. While on their knees the door opened and Ab. marched in— not drunk, but partially "under the influence."

"Hello Girls," he said, "put in a word for me while you're at it."

At the same time he knelt down beside them. The good ladies did not allow the interruption to interfere with their praying, and they did just what Ab. had asked—they put in a word for him. When they arose from their knees, they also had a few words with him. They told him about the meetings in the church and invited him to attend. To their surprise he readily consented, stipulating that some of the men call for him. The ladies with great enthusiasm reported their success to me that night at the meeting.

"What a glorious thing if he should be redeemed," said one, "you know I never saw his wife before today—but Mr. Coburn, her face shows the marks of a broken heart. I hear that Ab. isn't a bad fellow at all when sober, but when drunk he makes that home a hell."

At once I detailed two of my most reliable men to go to the Browne home the following evening and bring Ab. to the church. They reported to me that when they arrived they found Ab. at home and perfectly sober. When they stated their errand, he laughed heartily.

"Well this is some joke, Ab. Browne, the drunken fiddler goin' to a revival meetin'. I did promise them wimmen yesterday I'd go, and you know drunk or sober Ab. Browne's word is as good as his bond. So here goes, boys, I'll be with you in a minute."

When they arrived in sight of the church, however, Ab. stopped short: "Say boys, I wish you'd let me go back home and you apologize to the wimmen."

"Why Ab., what's the matter?"

"Well you see boys I've only been in church once in twenty-five years and that was to my mother's funeral. I don't know how to act, and I don't want to make a fool of myself."

"Now don't worry a bit about that, Ab.," said one of the men. "We'll sit in the back seat, and then you just stand up when the rest do and sit down when they sit. Come on man, don't back out now."

In that little church we had a good choir and fine singing. Ab. was passionately fond of music. He played the violin for dances all over the countryside. At the close of the service I made my way down to him.

"Good evening, sir, I think you're a stranger. I don't remember having seen you before. Might I ask your name?"

"Yes, sir, I'm a stranger in this church, although I don't live far from here. Browne—Ab. Browne is my name." We shook hands.

"Well, Mr. Browne, we're right glad to see you."

"Man but you've great singin' here—best bit o' singin' I've heard for many a day."

"Say Mr. Browne," I said, "there's an old saying—'One good turn deserves another', do you believe in it?"

"Of course I do."

"Are you prepared to practise it?"

"Yes, if it wouldn't be somethin' too hard to do."

"Oh this is easy—dead easy."

"O.K. what is it?"

"You came here tonight, that was one good turn. If you come back tomorrow night, that'll be another. Are you game?"

Ab. laughed. "Well, you're a rum one sure enough, but I'll be here, an' I'll tell the missus and the girls about the good singin' an' like as not they'll want to come too."

True to his word Ab. was on hand the following night. I shook hands with him as I did with the others and told him how glad we were to have him. The third night Ab. came again, this time accompanied by his wife. I concluded that the fish was nibbling at the hook but, afraid of losing him by too precipitate action, I made no further advance.

Then came the fourth night and there was Ab. in his old place in the back seat. In preparing and presenting the messages on these four nights, I am sure I had Ab. in my mind more than anyone else, and preached in such a way as I thought might help him. As I preached that fourth night I saw something in Ab's face that convinced me that the time for action had come. While the congregation was at prayer, led by one of my members, I slipped quietly down to Ab., and putting my hand on his shoulder, whispered in his ear:

"Ab., don't you think it's time for you to give yourself to God?"

"Yes, Mr. Coburn, that's what I want to do, but I don't know how. Will some one show me?"

I can never forget the thrill of that moment. "Come with me Ab." He followed—I led him up to the altar—the old fashioned "Penitent bench." I had no difficulty in getting him there, but it was not so easy to lead him into the "way." No man can completely neglect religion for twenty-five years, and then in a few moments leap into light. Ab's mind and soul were dark, but he was determined. For five nights he knelt at the altar. Sometimes the perspiration rolled from his forehead in a stream. Little by little, I helped him to see, that as he had done his part, the very best he knew how, and as he was willing to give up all his old evil ways, he must not doubt that God would do His. One night he said: "I believe it's a little brighter Mr. Coburn. I do believe."

Soon Ab. rose from the altar with a shining face and in very simple language told the people that he had given himself to Christ for life and that he believed God had accepted him, and that in his heart there was a peace and joy he had never known before.

The next morning, in Stayner, four and a half miles away, I met my friend the Chief of Police, Ben Cheeseman. Ben was a rough, good hearted fellow. He hailed me. "Say Coburn, I hear you got Ab. Browne last night, is it so?"

"Yes Ben, I'm glad to say it is true."

"Well by golly, that's a marvel. Say Parson, if you

keep that fellow sober for a week it's the greatest miracle that's ever happened around here."

"Ben," I replied, "Ab. Browne's going to be sober for the rest of his life."

"Ha, ha, ha—that's a good one. Say Coburn, you don't know your man. He's a holy terror. Honest to goodness, I'd rather handle any six men who come here than him when he's drunk. He's an awful decent fellow when sober— but drunk he's a devil. The worst of it is he's never sober long after he strikes town."

"Wait a minute, chief," I replied, "the man you are talking about died last night and a new Ab. Browne was born. That new man will get drunk no more."

The Chief just stood and stared at me for a few minutes. I am sure he thought that my common sense had deserted me. "Well, by golly, I hope you're right. The best of luck to you and him." But he turned away shaking his head.

That daring prophecy proved to be true. Ab. never drank again. He lived for eight beautiful, glorious years. His quiet, consistent Christian life was a mighty influence for good in the community. His years of dissipation, however, had undermined an otherwise strong constitution. He contracted a severe cold which developed into pneumonia and in a few days he died.

For some time previous to his death Ab. had taught a class of teen age girls in the Methodist Sunday School. The Sunday after his funeral, the Quarterly Communion and Reception service was held in the church. Every girl in Ab's class united with the church and received her first communion at that service.

I am now going to let Ab. tell his own story, he can do it so much better than I can. About six weeks after his conversion I was holding evangelistic meetings in the town church. I planned a meeting for men only on a Sunday afternoon. The local brass band was to be in attendance and we expected a full church. On the preceding Saturday afternoon I met Ab. on the street and said to him: "Ab. could you come tomorrow and tell these men what the Grace of God has done for you?"

"Why yes, Mr. Coburn, I'll be glad to, if you think it will do any good."

I was not prepared for what followed. My plan was simply to produce Ab. as an exhibit. The men all knew him and his former life. I wanted them to see what religion could do if people would give it a chance. I preached a short sermon and then called on Ab. to give his testimony. His language was very simple, he knew no other. But if real eloquence means the power to grip and hold the attention of an audience and to impress it with the truth of the statements and the sincerity of the speaker, then Ab. Browne's testimony that day was one of the most eloquent speeches to which I have ever listened.

"You fellows all know me," he began. "Time and again you've seen me roaming up and down these streets crazed with liquor. What you don't know, most of you anyway, is the awful thirst I had for the stuff. Men, I've gone out in the mornin' to the field to plow. When this thirst would come on me, I couldn't wait to put the horses in the stable. Often I've tied them to the fence and ran across the fields as hard as I could lick, until I got to a bar-room. When my wife rang the dinner bell, an' I didn't come, she knew, too well, what was the matter. She'd go out and get the horses and put them in the stable and feed them. Then she'd just go back to the house and wait. Sometimes she'd have to wait two or three days. It would depend on how much money I had. I've brought a load of grain to this town many a time and never left until every cent was spent. I don't know how my wife has put up with this as she has for years. She has suffered, my two girls have suffered, an' I've suffered myself. Time an' again I've told myself I was an awful fool, and I'd make up my mind to quit and be sober and sensible. But it was no good. That awful feelin' would get me. It's like a fire inside of you. I could do nothin'." Then he told of his being persuaded to attend services in the little church at Crow's Corners.

"While sittin' in that back seat in the church," he said, "I felt a terrible strong desire to be a better man, but I felt it was no use for me to try. Liquor had a real stranglehold on me. Other folks might be helped and saved, but not me. Then one night Mr. Coburn told us that God was Almighty and that He would help any fellow that was in dead earnest. He told us about a man in New York, Jerry McCauly, I think was his name. This guy, by all accounts was even worse than I was. He'd been in jail any number of times. Yet God saved him and made him a power to save others. So when Mr. Coburn came to me and said 'Come on Ab.', I made up my mind I'd give it a try anyway. I couldn't lose nothin'. It seemed too good to be true that a miserable critter like me could be saved. But there it was. The Bible said that He was able to save to the uttermost all that came to Him. Then I saw that meant me an' I said 'Lord I believe.' Then men, somethin' happened, I don't know what, but I felt free and happy like. A nice feelin' of rest and peace came over me, an' it was like someone said—'It's all right Ab.' My wife and two daughters came forward and found Christ too. I think we have the happiest family in the Township of Sunnidale. Mr. Coburn advised me to set up a family altar. I didn't know what he meant but he explained and so mornin' and night we have our little Bible readin' and prayer. But the strangest thing of all, men, is what has happened to this thirst for liquor. It's gone. You know I expected to have a stiff fight over that. For days I was afraid to come to town. One day I had to go into one of the hotels on business an' I shook all over. I was afraid that if I got a whiff of the smell of the stuff, it would bring on the old thing. But nothin' happened. I met men with the smell of it on their breath, but it means nothin' to me. I guess God saw that I wasn't strong enough to put up much of a fight, so he just stepped in an' took the desire clean away. Since that night when I found peace in Bethseda Church, until now, I haven't for one minute had the slightest desire for a drink. Am I thankful?—well you can just bet I am—I've had more real happiness in the past six weeks than in all my life before. An' I believe that the Grace of God that has done this for me, can also keep me. Men, I've signed on with Jesus Christ for life."

At the conclusion of the service one of my officials and a very close friend came to me and said: "Well Coburn, this is one time when you've been put completely in the shade. I guess that sermon of yours was O.K. but I don't think anyone remembers a word of it. Ab. stole the show. I tell you a testimony like that is worth a hundred sermons." And so said we all.

In that simple faith Ab. lived and died. A couple of years after his conversion he sold his farm and bought a market garden within the town limits. He was the principal factor in closing the three bar-rooms and liquor store by Local Option. I had tried to do so but failed. Ab. took the petition from house to house. To those who hesitated to sign he would say: "Come now, you know what booze did to me—it's doin' the same to other poor devils. Let's put it out of business and give them a chance."

That Local Option law still stands. For over forty years, largely through Ab's instrumentality Stayner has been dry.

9

HERE COMES THE BRIDE

1. *Spit on it, Bill*

ON ONE of my circuits there was an appointment whose members and adherents were mostly north of Ireland folk or their children. They were a happy, carefree lot. Social gatherings were usually scenes of hilarity and innocent mischief. I was told that on one occasion at an old fashioned tea meeting in the church, after supper, at the opening of the programme, a visiting parson was asked to offer a prayer. This good man's terminal facilities were very poor so his prayer became long and wearisome for the young bloods in the back seats. At its conclusion they gave him an encore.

These same people gave me the greatest difficulty in closing a service with proper decorum. It was only by a tremendous effort I managed to keep a straight face and steady voice. In addition, I had to try to control the mirth of the crowd.

It was a wedding, in a large, old-fashioned farm house, the house of a little mite of a man, named Hercules Ritchie. Hercules' daughter, Caroline, was being married to the son of a neighbour and fellow officer of the little church, named Bill Campbell. Everybody for miles around was there—the women in their very best finery, the men in their Sunday suits, most of them horribly uncomfortable in their starched linen collars. All were duly impressed with the importance and solemnity of the occasion and so attempted a formality of behaviour which was far from their usual mode of life.

Bill and Caroline were most estimable young people highly respected by all. They were both active in the Church and took a leading part in the work of the Epworth League. Some austere and cynical church members used to allege that "that Epworth League is only a sparking school anyway." The charge was only partially true. The League did much more than afford facilities for romance. But it was a sparking school and a very good one at that. Many a man (including the writer) did a lot of his courting on the way to and from the meetings of the Epworth League. The kind of mate one found there would probably be much superior to that found in certain other places of social resort.

Bill and Caroline had known each other from childhood. It was no hasty "love at first sight" affair. Neither was it a marriage of convenience. While the parents on both sides cordially approved, it was wholly a matter of Bill and Caroline's choice—a genuine love match. At last the great moment arrived and they stood before the minister to be made one for life.

As is usually the case on such occasions, Bill was far more nervous than his bride. All went well, however, until the time arrived for placing the ring on the bride's finger. Bill was having some difficulty in getting the ring past the knuckle. Whether that was due to the ring being a trifle small, the bride's finger a little moist, or to Bill's nervousness, I don't know. At any rate, Bill with his big fists, was striving manfully to get the job done. I was afraid that in his eagerness he might tear the girl's finger, so said *sotto voce:* "Take your time, Bill, take your time." There was a silence in which the ticking of the clock could be heard as the people watched the proceedings. Poor Bill's face was getting redder every minute. Then from away back in the crowd, a male voice spoke up helpfully: "Spit on it, Bill."

The whole group burst into loud laughter. I had the greatest difficulty in sobering them down so that I could finish the service decently and in order. Two or three times they became quiet, when someone would give a snort or a giggle. Away they would go again. However, the job was finally completed. That was nearly fifty years ago and Bill and Caroline have lived happily together ever since.

2. *A Bedside Wedding and Baptism*

One morning in 1909 on answering the summons of the door bell of the old Parliament Street Church parsonage in Toronto, I found a young man with a most woe-begone countenance.

"You're the minister, aren't you, sir?"

"Yes, I am a minister."

"Well, mister, I'm in terrible trouble."

"Come right in then," I said. After getting him seated I asked him what was the matter.

"It's me and my girl, sir, we've been in love for a long time, and we planned to get married as soon as we had enough money to set up a home. But mister, we done wrong, we let our feelings get the better of us, and we done what we shouldn't. And mister, last night she had a baby. And believe me mister, I didn't know a thing about it. She never let me know. If I'd only known, sir, I'd a married her right off, money or no money. But she kept it dark. Now I want to marry her just as soon as I can. Could you please come and marry us today?"

"Where is she?" I inquired.

"She has been working as a maid for a very nice woman up on Delaware Avenue. The woman is very kind. They are taking good care of her. There's a nurse looking after her and the baby."

"Well now, young man, I admire your eagerness to get this thing squared away as quickly as possible, but as I am the father of four children I am perhaps better posted in this business than you are. A girl who had a baby last night, will scarcely be in very good condition for a wedding today. If you give me the telephone number, I will talk to the nurse. She will be able to advise us."

When I called the nurse and explained the situation she burst into a merry laugh: "That's pretty good, don't you think so, sir?" Yes, I thought it was.

"Well," she said, "the girl and the baby are fine—as well as could be expected, but you know having a baby is quite a shock to the system under the best of conditions. It will be much better if you can persuade him to wait until tomorrow at least."

"All right, nurse, I'm quite sure that is sound advice. If all is well, how about two-thirty tomorrow?"

"Very good," she replied.

"Then nurse, unless I hear from you that further delay is advisable we'll be there tomorrow at two-thirty. Will you please notify the girl and also the lady of the house? I will need two witnesses. I suggest you and the lady of the house act in that capacity. We don't want to embarrass the young people by having more people around than is necessary."

"Very well, sir, if in the morning I think the girl is not strong enough, I will 'phone you."

When I told the young man, he said: "Well sir, of course, if it's for her good, I'll wait, but I do want to get married to her as soon as I can. You know, sir, I love her an awful lot and I wouldn't do anything to hurt her for all the world. It was all my fault, sir. I don't want you to think that Nellie is a bad girl. She isn't, sir. The only thing she done wrong is that she didn't slap my face and tell me if I couldn't behave I could go about my business."

While this speech was in progress the boy was diligently

wiping away the tears that were running down his cheeks. I asked him his name and address and instructed him about getting a marriage license. He and I had an interesting conversation that morning. He told me of his home and early life, but every little while he would revert to the present situation and express his regret for what had happened.

"I could kick myself into the middle of next week."

He told me how he came to Toronto to get a job and how lonely he was. Then he met Nellie. She was lonely too. He said they quickly fell for each other. Then nothing else mattered.

I told him how much I appreciated his attitude and especially his desire to rectify the situation as far as possible.

"Of course," I said, "it cannot be denied that you have sinned grievously, both of you. You both knew better, but you must not allow this sense of sin and remorse for the past to get you down. Remember there is forgiveness for sin. 'Though your sins be as scarlet, they shall be white as snow.' If you attempted to brazen this thing out, defend and make excuses for your conduct, I would have little hope for you. But you have been ready to acknowledge your fault, and make it right. That is the manly, the Christian thing to do. In spite of this mistake, there is no reason why you and your girl may not build up a good home and worthy lives. You will have each other. From what you have told me you love each other very much. That will help a lot. Then you will have a dear little child, your very own. Together you will watch it grow and develop. It may sometimes bring anxiety to you. That too will bind you together. Then, my boy, above all, you can have the Grace of God that will never fail you. Don't worry any more about the past. The future is bright."

He shook my hand and said: "Thank you sir, thank you. I feel a lot better already. I wish you'd talk a little like that to Nellie tomorrow. I'm a bit afraid she'll be feeling blue, and that we have so disgraced ourselves that there isn't much hope for us."

"All right, Jim," I said. "You'd better telephone me about noon tomorrow and if all is well, we'll meet at Delaware Avenue at 2.30 p.m. Goodbye for now."

So, the next day, not having heard from the nurse, I presented myself at the door of the Delaware Avenue home, a little before two-thirty. The lady of the house received me very graciously. In the course of our conversation I remarked that the one thing I couldn't understand was that the young man didn't "catch on" as to how matters stood.

"Perhaps," she said, "you won't wonder so much at that, when I tell you, that that girl fooled me as completely as she did her young man. I have been married for years, and have two children of my own, but believe me I hadn't the slightest suspicion that anything like this was afoot until a few minutes before the baby was born. Nellie has been with us for over a year, and no one could wish for a better maid. She is quiet and modest. She never stayed out to an unseemly hour as so many girls do nowadays. This young man was very attentive to her. He seemed to be a nice boy and so far as I could see their behaviour was all that anyone could desire."

"It must have been quite a shock to you," I said.

"Indeed it was," she continued, "yesterday after lunch the girl took very sick. I saw she was in great pain. She couldn't hide that. I sent her to bed and 'phoned the doctor. He came and after visiting her in her room, came out with a funny smile on his face. 'Why didn't you tell me you were staging a show like this?' he asked.

" 'Staging a show, what on earth do you mean, and what are you grinning about? That's a sick girl in there if I'm any judge.'

" 'Oh, don't worry,' said he, 'she'll be all right soon.'

" 'I hope so,' I returned, 'what's the matter with her?'

" 'Mrs. Roberts, you don't mean to tell me you don't know what is the matter?'

" 'I certainly don't know. That's why I sent for you. Now please get that silly grin off your face and tell me—if you know.' I was fast losing my patience. Then he told me. I just couldn't believe it. 'Impossible doctor,' I said.

" 'No mam, not only possible but actual.'

"Then I confess for a moment or two I saw red, to think that immoral conduct had been carried on in my house. 'Well doctor, you better get her to a hospital or some other place.'

" 'I'm afraid it's a little too late, Mrs. Roberts. I am quite sure that before I could get an ambulance here the baby will have arrived.'

"Then Mr. Coburn, I had another thought. Suppose this girl was my own, and was away among strangers in a big city, with no mother or other friend near her, what would I want another woman to do for her? That settled it.

" 'All right, doctor, she can stay. You'll need a nurse won't you?'

" 'Well, we'd be the better for one for a few days,' he replied.

" 'Well, then, 'phone the hospital and get one.'

"I made up my mind that when I got my hands on that young fellow I'd give him such a piece of my mind that he'd never forget. I 'phoned him at once and told him to get over as fast as he could. He came on the run, thinking his Nellie must be dying or something of that sort. But I found the fellow was as greatly surprised as I was. At once he acknowledged that he was to blame, and he seemed so distressed and repentant, that I couldn't find it in my heart to say a word to him."

"What does your husband say to all this?" I asked.

"I didn't know just how he would take it. He is a good living man and with very strict ideas on moral questions. He has a hot temper, too, but beneath it all a kind heart.

So when he came home last night I broke the news to him as tactfully as I could. At first he wouldnt' believe it. He thought I was pulling some sort of a joke on him. He didn't like it either. 'Nellie's too nice a girl to say anything like that about her even in fun,' he said.

"Then the baby upstairs gave a lusty cry. That convinced him. He flared up for a minute, declaring he would have no such goings on in his house. Then I went upstairs and brought down the baby and laid it in his arms. I knew his weak spot. He is just crazy about children. He looked down at the little face and said: 'Poor wee kiddie, we couldn't throw you out on the street, could we?'

"Then suddenly he threw back his head and roared with laughter. You know John has a great sense of humour. He can see a funny side in almost any situation. 'Mary,' he said, 'this is a whale of a joke. To think that an old married woman, mother of two children could be fooled so completely by a slip of a girl—ho, ho, ho;' and away he went into another spasm. 'I never thought my wife would be so dumb, ho, ho, ho.' Then, 'How's Nellie, is she all right?'

" 'Just fine, John.'

" 'Well I'd like to wring that young villain Jim's neck.'

" 'No John, he was as much in the dark as I was. He is very penitent, and John he is bringing a minister to marry them as soon as possible.'

" 'Well, Mary, you did the right thing—the only thing you could do. God is merciful to sinners, and we ought to be too.' "

In due time Jim arrived and we all went upstairs to where the bride-to-be was lying. She was in a lovely, bright room with every comfort. Jim stood close to the bedside and I married them. Without being told to do so, at the conclusion of the ceremony, he stooped down and kissed her. It was no mere matter of form either.

When I was preparing the certificate and registration papers, the bride called her husband over to her bedside.

They held a brief whispered conversation, when Jim approached me: "Mr. Coburn, would it be in order for you to baptize the baby too?"

"Would you like me to?" I asked.

"Yes sir, if you please. You see we have no regular church. Our homes are quite a distance in different directions from Toronto. We've just been going to one church and another. We went to your church sometimes, but I guess you don't remember us. I went to you about getting married because you were a young man. I thought maybe you'd understand better than the older men."

"Well, have you a name for the baby?"

"Oh, yes, we have a name."

Jim insisted that the wee girl be named after her mother Helen. Nellie then spoke up: "Mrs. Roberts has been so good to us, that if she doesn't object I would like to call her Mary."

Mrs. Roberts gave full consent. So Helen Mary it was.

The nurse brought in a little water from which the chill had been taken and I baptized the baby. As Jim had suggested, I had a little chat with them and offered a prayer. They promised me that when they established their home they would connect themselves with some church, try to make their home a Christian one and bring up their little one in the best possible way.

In my time, I have officiated at a great many weddings. On some occasions the ceremony was held in a church, with great banks of flowers, and a crowd of well-dressed men and women, and at the home after a magnificent display of costly presents. But I declare I never went away from a marriage service with more pleasant feelings than I did that day. Everybody concerned had acted splendidly.

10

THE RUNAWAYS

1. *A Mixed Marriage Affair*

In 1908 the Pope of Rome promulgated what was called the
Ne Temere decree. It forbade Roman Catholics to marry
Protestants except with the permission of the Church and
by one of its own priests. For a Roman Catholic to be
married to a Protestant by a Protestant minister was not
only no marriage in the eyes of the Church, but was a
grievous sin. Fierce controversy raged over this decree and
it was the cause of much trouble in the homes of Roman
Catholics and Protestants among young people who did not
allow denominational lines to interfere with their love
affairs.

At this time I was pastor of Parliament Street
Methodist Church in Toronto. The parsonage was an old
established one and consequently many strangers came to
the minister to be married. One evening a young man called
and inquired if I could marry a couple the following Saturday night at the parsonage. I agreed to do so and asked
if he would have witnesses or if I would have to provide
them. He seemed a bit startled and said:

"No, we won't bring any witnesses."

Something in his manner aroused my suspicion. "Say, my boy is this a runaway affair?" said I.

After a moment's hesitation he replied: "Well, yes, I guess you might call it that."

"I'm afraid I'll have to ask you to tell me all about it."

"Well, sir, it's this way. My girl is a Roman Catholic and I am a Protestant. I have boarded in her father's home for six months. They are just the finest people in the world, but very strict Catholics. Whatever their Church says is law to them. The girl and I are terribly in love. We just can't bear to think of anything ever coming between us. We know that if we told them we wanted to get married there would be an awful row. That old man would order me from the house and forbid us ever to see each other again. So, as we have fully decided to live our own lives in our own way, we are going to get married. Then what is done can't be undone. We know they'll be awful mad, but they are warm hearted Irish people and they are very fond of their daughter. She's just the apple of her father's eye. So we hope that after a while they will accept the situation and forgive us. At any rate the girl says she loves me enough to run all risks, even if her folks never speak to her again."

"How old is she?"

"Twenty past, sir."

"Are you absolutely sure of that?"

"Oh, yes sir, I have heard her parents tell things that showed that is her age right enough."

"Another question. Does she clearly understand that if I marry you, she puts herself right out of the Catholic Church?"

"Yes sir, we've gone all over that. She is willing to come with me."

"You need to be sure of that. You know there have been a number of cases in which people have been married under similar circumstances and all went well for a while.

Then a priest tells the wife that in God's sight there is no marriage at all and that she is living in open sin and in danger of hell fire. The Church's hold on the minds of most Catholics is a strong one. In some of the cases the wife has insisted on another marriage by a priest. The husband has refused thus to declare openly that he and his wife have been living in sin and their children are illegitimate. So bitter strife has arisen in the home, and in some cases separation has taken place. Now you see how serious this is. You and this young woman are running a serious risk. We must be sure that she thoroughly understands what it involves."

"I think she does sir, and I am sure no priest could come between us."

"Well, I hope so. I can promise you one thing. If she doesn't understand now, she will by the time I have finished with her. Before I perform the marriage ceremony under such circumstances, I will feel it my duty to explain everything to her and to exact from her a most solemn promise never even to discuss the validity of her marriage with anyone and never to demand from you any other ceremony."

"That'll be fine, sir. I think she understands but it will do no harm for you to put the matter good and strong."

At the appointed time the young people came. I found the girl a very bright, attractive person and evidently much in love with her young man. I found she was quite clear about the Church's attitude. She said she couldn't believe there was only one way to Heaven, that she had a lot of Protestant friends whom she was sure were good people. She didn't believe that the Catholic Church was the only true church. With her lover (unknown to her parents) she had gone several times to Protestant Churches. She liked the service.

"One thing," she said, "I could understand it all. The Catholic Service is in Latin, and I don't know what it's all about. I'm quite willing to go with Jim." She readily promised that no one would be allowed to interfere with their marriage.

I married them.

On the following Monday morning I attended the Ministerial Association. On returning home, when I came in sight of the parsonage I saw a little old man at the door talking to my wife. As I came near I heard her say: "Oh, here he is now."

When I came up the steps the visitor in a rich Irish brogue asked: "Are you the minister sorr?"

"I am."

"Was" (giving the names) "here on Saturday night to get married"?

"Yes, they were here."

"And av coorse you didn't marry them?"

"And of course I did."

"How dare you, sorr? You didn't take time to inquire and find out that the girl is undther age." Then the old man poured out a perfect torrent of curses and abuse. He was really eloquent. When he paused for breath I managed to inject: "You say the girl is under age. How old is she?"

"She's only twenty, sorr, and you ought to have known better than marry such a pair. A nice article you are, calling yourself a minister." Away he went again, winding up with this climax: "I'll pray God to curse every bone in your durty damned carcass."

I told him that he was mistaken, that a girl of twenty had full legal right to marry with or without her parents' consent, that the young people seemed to understand fully what they were doing, and that as there was no legal or moral reason why they should not marry if they so desired, I had married them. I urged him to make the best of it, allowing the young folk to live their own lives in their own way.

He just glared at me and turned away. I stood in the door and watched him go. Two or three times before he passed out of sight he turned and shook his clenched fist in my direction. Then along came a young girl, whom I could see had been crying. She was very much excited. She asked me if that old man had been speaking to me. When I replied in the affirmative she said: "He's my father. He's awful mad. We were afraid he might do something awful. Are you the minister?"

"Yes, I'm the minister."

"Did you marry my sister?"

"I believe I did."

Going down the steps she said: "I want to keep father in sight, but I don't want him to see me." When she got to the sidewalk she turned to me and said: "Are you sure you married them?"

"Yes, my girl, perfectly sure."

"Oh dear, oh dear, what'll we do?"

She walked slowly down the street after her father. Next morning the old man returned. I happened to be downtown and my wife answered the door.

"Is his riverence in, ma'am,"

"No, Mr. Coburn is downtown somewhere."

"Well, I'm sorry, ma'am. I cam to ax his pardon for what I said till him yesterday. You know ma'am, it's the awfullest blow me and me ould woman ever got. We have thried to be good Catholics all our lives. Our Church taiches that that marriage is no marriage at all, at all. That bein' so then our daughter is livin' in open sin and our whole family is disgraced. An' I'm tellin' you ma'am, that our family has always been dassint and respectable. Nothing like this has ever happened to us affore. An' to think that my own Judy would go and do this to her ould dad and mother. That girl was my favourite. I loved her like no one else. An' just to think of her livin' with that fellow in sin—the durty spalpeen, oid like to wring his neck. Oh, ma'am, you bein' a Protestant'll not know what this manes to us. But, ma'am, when I got home and cooled off and the mad went off me a bit I could see that his riverence wasn't to blame. I had no business talkin' to him the way I did. So, ma'am, will you plaze tell his riverence I'm sorry and ax him to forgive me for all the bad things I said till him."

The old man had wept copiously as he spoke and my wife admitted that she could very easily have dropped a few tears over the sorrows of this old man, ignorant, simple and violent, but sincere and loyal to what he believed to be the right.

2. *A Captain's Daughter and a Bank Clerk*

STAYNERITIS—This word in large capital letters was the heading of a full page advertisement of Beggs and Company, General Merchants, appearing in an issue of the Collingwood *Bulletin*. During recent months there had been a series of elopements from Collingwood. A number of young couples, without the knowledge or consent of parents or of anyone else, had quietly driven over to Stayner, ten miles away and had been married by one of the Stayner ministers. In this rather unique advertisement Begg and Company declared that any young people developing symptoms of *Stayneritis* would do well to consult them. In their store were to be found all the requisites—wedding garments for both bride and groom, furniture and other household supplies. They would be glad to furnish the nest with goods of the best quality and at the very lowest prices.

One cold, stormy night, a horse and cutter drove up to my door, and in came a young man and a very beautiful and charming girl. The young man Bob Winters presented a marriage license and asked me to marry them. Noting that the license gave their residence as Collingwood, I was a little suspicious and said:

"This isn't by any chance a run-away affair, is it?"

They were a little startled and confused by my question. Finally the young man admitted that it was.

"Then you must tell me, why the rush and the secrecy," I said.

"Well, sir, it's this way," said Winters, "I'm a bank clerk and I may be moved at any time. Mary and I are much in love and we are afraid if we are separated something might prevent our marriage later. Perhaps you know, sir, that bank clerks are not allowed to marry until they are receiving a certain salary. If the bank found out I had married, I would be dismissed. So if you please, sir, will you keep our secret for us?"

"Is that the whole story?"

"No," said the young lady, Mary Wilson, "my chief reason is on account of my father."

"Your father, who is he?"

"Captain Peter Wilson."

"Captain Wilson of the *North Star?*"

"Yes, sir."

I knew Captain Peter well. He was a competent sailor, but one of the most vile tempered, profane men I ever met. He was a tyrant and a bully. If the slightest thing on the ship displeased him he would fly into a rage and pour out a torrent of profane abuse on all concerned. It was said that he could curse and swear for a longer time without repeating himself than any man who sailed the lakes. He was also a notorious liar. It was his great delight to get two or three lady passengers into his cabin and horrify them with tales of a most gruesome and blood curdling character. So I said to the young lady:

"Very well, Miss Wilson, what about your father?"

"In many ways he is a good father. But he seems to think he has the right to boss the lives of his children. He made my sister Edith give up a nice boy with whom she was in love and marry a rich man. She had a great wedding and went on her honeymoon on a special train but I know

her heart was broken. She lives in a fine home with everything that money can buy but she is unhappy. Father
warned me to quit seeing Bob and told me he was planning
to get me a good rich husband like Edith. He means well,
I know, but I'll not let him ruin my life as he has my
sister's. I'm going to marry the man I love."

"How old are you?"

"Twenty, sir."

"Does your mother know about this? Does she approve?"

"Yes, sir."

"And so do I my girl, I glory in your spunk."

"Mr. Coburn," Mary said, "just one thing troubles me.
The Bible says, 'Children, obey your parents.' You don't
think I'm doing wrong, do you?"

"My dear girl, you have made a mistake often made by
people quoting scripture. You have quoted only a part of
the verse. It says 'Children, obey your parents in the Lord.'
I am very sure the Lord has no part in the tyranny your
father is trying to exercise on you."

Her face lit up with a radiant smile.

"Oh, thank you sir, so much. You've made me very
happy."

So I married them. As soon as I had pronounced the
"Amen" of the Benediction, they literally flung themselves
into each others arms. I never saw a newly married pair
more deliriously happy than were they. Of course, Mary
had to go back to her home and Bob to his boarding house.
Only the mother and the folks in the parsonage shared their
great secret. Some months elapsed during which Bob often
went to the Wilson home when Captain Peter was away.
But the time came when both mother and daughter felt
that he should be told. The great question was how to
break the news to him. Both dreaded it as they were quite
sure it would result in a violent scene.

Next door to the Wilsons, a family named Jenkins lived.
Mr. Jenkins and the Captain were close friends. About a

year before, Jenkins' daughter had eloped with a young fellow and was married by the Presbyterian minister in Stayner. Jenkins was not as hot tempered as was Wilson, but he was greatly upset. Strange to say the Captain at Mrs. Jenkins' request acted as peacemaker and with fair success. In a short time Jenkins became reconciled to the situation, and received his new son-in-law into the family circle. Mrs. Wilson and Mary decided to ask Mr. Jenkins to perform the same service as the Captain had performed for him. He readily agreed.

"It'll be great fun handing back to the old rascal some of the same dose he gave me over Jenny."

Mr. Jenkins knew his man and laid his plans carefully. He was a cattle buyer. So one day he said to his friend: "Captain, I have to go to Singhampton tomorrow to buy some cattle, come along with me for the ride."

The Captain agreed and they drove out with a horse and buggy. When they arrived Jenkins broke the news. He thought that an hour and a half's drive over the rough country road would give the Captain time to cool off. The Captain as expected was furious. There was no vile name in his extensive vocabulary that he didn't apply to Bob Winters.

"And to think that my daughter, my own flesh and blood would do this to me, the ungrateful little hussy. I've done everything for her, given her everything she asked for. Well, she's made her bed, now she can lie in it. From this on she's no daughter of mine. I never want to see her face again and as for that bank clerk, he'd better keep out of my reach or I'll wring his neck."

Jenkins did his best to abate the old man's wrath but to no avail. He didn't have the fun he anticipated. When he ventured to remind the Captain of the things he had said when the situation was reversed, he turned savagely on him:

"And so you, too, have turned against me. I didn't

expect it of you, Jenkins. If you and I are to be friends, you better keep out of this. I'll settle this affair in my own way. When I walk the bridge of my ship I'm Master and in my house I'll be the same or know the reason why."

On and on he went, cursing, swearing and threatening. When he arrived at his home he demanded that Mary come to him at once. He repeated all the things he had said to Jenkins on the way home and much more. He ordered her to pack her things and get out of his house and never return.

"And tell that young skunk, I suppose you call him husband now, he'd better keep clear of me."

Mary, of course, was not surprised but very sorry. In spite of his bad temper, she loved her father. Mrs. Wilson felt the separation from her daughter keenly but she comforted Mary as best she could. She told her that her father's attitude was caused by the extreme poverty of his own family. "Polly," he said, "One thing I've set my mind on. No child of mine will ever go through what I did as a boy." Mrs. Wilson assured her that it would all work out in the end. Little did she think of the strange means by which her prophecy was to come true.

The immediate result, however, was that Bob Winters lost his job. The irate Captain did not keep his grievance a secret. Next day he told some of his cronies what his ungrateful daughter had done to him. The news soon spread over town. When the bank authorities heard of it they dismissed Bob immediately. Fortunately he was able to secure an equally good position almost at once.

Some months later the Captain took sick. He became so ill that for a time his life hung in the balance. However, he had a good strong constitution and with skilled medical care and efficient nursing he pulled through. But he had had a pretty bad scare and as he lay in bed for weeks had ample opportunity for reflection. During his convalescence he sent a message to Mary asking her to come to see him and to bring her husband with her. Very gladly they complied. He had given instructions to his wife that when they arrived she was to send Bob up first—alone. When Bob arrived he found the old man in bed propped up with pillows in a partially sitting posture. As soon as Bob entered the room the Captain began a tirade the like of which poor Bob had never had directed at him before. The Captain cursed and swore with more than his usual eloquence then said:

"Over there in the drawer in that wash stand there's a cheque book and a fountain pen, bring them to me."

Bob did as he was bidden. The old man wrote out a cheque for five hundred dollars, gave it to Bob saying:

"There, take that, and go downstairs and send that other damned fool up."

When Mary came into his room she was shocked at the appearance of her father. He had lost a lot of flesh and his face was almost without colour but she soon found that his mind was as active and his tongue as sharp as ever. He gave her a dose fully equal in virulence to the one he had just given her husband. Then he handed her a cheque for five hundred dollars and bade her get out and let him get some sleep. Just as she reached the door, however, he called her:

"Come here girl, right over here close. Mary, would you mind giving your old Dad a bit of a kiss?"

Mary was startled. Not since she was a little girl had he ever done such a thing. However, she bent over and kissed him. As she did so, he flung both arms around her and pressed her to him.

"You gol blasted little hussy you, you're the only one on sea or land who ever disobeyed me and got away with it. I'm damned if I'm not proud of you. You're a chip off the old block."

11

THE FIGHT FOR A CLEAN STAGE

1. *The Star Theatre*

Brrr—went the telephone in the old Parliament Street Parsonage one Saturday afternoon. A man who refused to give his name, informed me that he and a friend had attended a performance in the *Star Theatre* the previous evening and found it to be indescribably filthy and obscene. I had never visited the *Star* but knew its reputation as the number one purveyor of indecency in the city. It was patronized almost exclusively by men and boys. If a woman appeared, it was a foregone conclusion that she belonged to a certain type.

I decided to investigate my unknown informant's complaint. From his story and the general reputation of the place, I was prepared for a pretty rough show but I had never imagined such a scene possible in "Toronto the Good." It was shamelessly obscene.

On Monday morning I went down to the office of Rev. Dr. Chown, Secretary of the Board of Temperance, Prohibition and Moral Reform of the Methodist Church. I told him of my experience.

"Coburn, this is splendid," he said.

"Splendid, why man it was awful."

Laughing heartily he replied: "Oh, don't get me wrong.

I didn't mean that that show was splendid. Far from it. I have known for some time that place is one of the most vicious things in our city life. But for you to have seen it, and to be able to give such a clear and detailed description is splendid. It's just what I have been wanting. Now, you know Judge Winchester?"

"Yes, Doctor, I know him very well. He is an elder in Parkdale Presbyterian Church and a fine man."

"Yes and he is also Chairman of the Board of Police Commissioners for Toronto."

Dr. Chown called the judge who invited us to go to his office at once, where I gave him the information I had given Dr. Chown.

"Thank you, Mr. Coburn," he said, "I have been convinced for a long time that that place was a hot bed of indecency but as I had no definite proof, I have been unable to persuade my two colleagues on the Board to consent to closing it up. The Board meets tomorrow. Will you come and just report word for word what you have told me?"

"I'll be glad to do that Your Honour, if it will do any good."

"Do any good! I wonder what Mayor Oliver and Colonel Denison will say when they hear this! By the way Dr. Chown, can you come with Mr. Coburn? It will give him some moral support. He is a young man, but you have experience and your official position gives you authority. For myself I believe every word Coburn has said. It fits in with other information that has come to me. But I know these other men are going to get a shock."

Dr. Chown and I appeared as requested. For the third time I went over the noxious tale. The Mayor got quite excited. "You should have gone right up on the stage and dragged these creatures off and broken up the show."

"Now, now Mr. Oliver, Mr. Coburn would have been very wrong if he had done what you suggest, and would probably have been arrested by one of our police for being a public nuisance," said Judge Winchester. "Dr. Chown and Mr. Coburn have done the proper thing. They came to me yesterday. I asked them to come here today. We are the men responsible for conditions in our city. They have done as good citizens should, placed the information in our hands."

He turned to us, "Thank you, gentlemen. I assure you the matter will receive immediate attention."

The same afternoon I was called and informed that Inspector Stevens, head of the Morality Department, wanted to see me. I went to his office and found an old man partially decrepit through rheumatism, a canny Scotsman, a police officer of the old school. I introduced myself.

"Oh, you're Mr. Coburn?" looking me up and down.

"Yes, sir."

"I understand Mr. Coburn that you were before the Board of Police Commissioners today?"

"Yes sir, Dr. Chown and I were there on the request of the Chairman, Judge Winchester."

"Yes, yes, I know all about that. Now will you please be good enough to tell me what you told them."

"Certainly sir."

So for the fourth time, the tale was told. I confess I was getting a bit sick of it. When I had finished the inspector said: "I suppose you know that all theatres are under my supervision. An officer visits each one at the first performance on Monday, and if he sees anything that is objectionable, he orders it cut out. Now what day did you say this occurred?"

"Last Saturday afternoon, sir."

The Inspector called for the file and produced the police officer's report.

"Yes, I see that our officer was there on the Monday previous. This is his report. I'll read it to you." The officer had ordered the deletion of three minor items and made no reference to the things that I reported.

"This officer is good, a man of experience, I don't know what to think about it." Then turning to me and looking steadily in my face he said: "Now Mr. Coburn, I have a straight question to ask you, are you prepared to go into court and make these statements under oath?"

"Certainly sir," I replied.

"Oh ye are, are ye?"

"Well, why not? Of course I'll go to court if asked."

"Well then, that bein' the case, I am instructed to prosecute, but of course, I don't expect we'll win."

"Why not?" I asked. "Can things like that go on and nothing be done?"

"Well, well, we'll see. You'll get your summons as a witness in due time."

"I'll be on hand sir, when I'm wanted."

If Inspector Stevens had had his way, we might not have won. He planned to call his own officer first, and have him tell what he saw on Monday. His tale would doubtless have been in line with his report. Then I was to be called to tell what I saw on Saturday. If the Magistrate believed my story, it would mean that the theatre added the objectionable items after the officer's visit. If the manager of the theatre were convicted the Morality Department of the Police Force would be relieved of blame.

The Crown Attorney was Mr. J. W. S. Corley, K.C., an able lawyer, by no means a puritan, but honest and efficient in his work.

"No, Inspector," he said, "we'll not do that at all. Mr. Coburn has taken the responsibility of coming forward and giving this information. I will put him in the box first and have him tell his story. Then I will call your officer and take him over Coburn's story point by point."

That was done. Under oath the unhappy witness had to admit that practically everything I saw on Saturday he had seen on Monday. Thus my evidence was corroborated. By Steven's plan much of my evidence would have been uncorroborated. Witnesses could doubtless have been produced by the defence who would have denied my statements. Under these conditions acquittal would have been highly probable. At the conclusion of the testimony, the Magistrate asked him:

"Officer, why didn't you order all these things cut out of that show?"

He replied:

"To tell the truth your Worship, there was a streak of filth runnin' all through that show, like a scarlet thread in a web of cloth. The only way to destroy the thread is to destroy the web. The only way I could have cleaned up that show was to close it up."

"And that is precisely what you should have done," said the Magistrate.

The reader can form some estimate of the character of the show by the fact that in reporting the case, *The Toronto Evening Telegram* stated: "From this point on Mr. Coburn's evidence is simply unprintable." That statement was not an exaggeration.

One incident of the trial furnished much enjoyed amusement to the Magistrate. He delighted above all things in a good joke on a lawyer. I heard him once completely flatten out one of Toronto's most prominent K.C.'s. On this occasion the Star Theatre had secured Mr. J. W. Curry to defend it. Mr. Curry was the lawyer for the wet interests in the famous battle in the Court of Revision before Judge Winchester during the campaign to close forty bars, a story I have told elsewhere in this book. As there was no doubt that we had far the best of the encounter, Mr. Curry had the memories of an enemy and a worsted one at that.

When I had finished my evidence in chief, Mr. Curry proceeded to cross-examine me.

"Now Mr. Coburn, you have a rather poor memory, haven't you?"

"Why no, Mr. Curry, I have a fairly good memory—at least I have always thought so."

"No, no, I don't agree. You remember the battle you and I had before Judge Winchester at the Court of Revision?"

"I certainly do, sir."

"Well then you remember that you made a lot of statements and that I put witnesses in the box who contradicted you?"

"But Mr. Curry, you will no doubt remember that Judge Winchester didn't believe either you or your witnesses."

The Magistrate, though on the bench, laughed heartily as did many in the courtroom.

After a few perfunctory questions Mr. Curry desisted. The Magistrate promptly found the manager of the theatre guilty of the charge but fined him only $10.00 and costs. That penalty was woefully inadequate. The unsavoury show had been repeated twice a day for six days. The attendance would run from five hundred to a thousand each time. The Magistrate who had this case was one of Toronto's most highly respected citizens, and had a fine sense of what was moral and decent. He could be relied on to give a fair and sound decision on the facts of such a case. But like some of his colleagues, he did not seem to regard such an offence with sufficient seriousness. If some poor chap had stolen a few dollars, and had been convicted in the Toronto police court, he would probably be sent to jail for a good stiff term, but a man could corrupt the morals of thousands and escape with a ten dollar fine.

2. *The Forty Thieves*

Some time after my first visit to the Star Theatre, a Congregational minister named St. Clair, who was living in Toronto, dropped into the Star one day and found a show quite the equal in indecency with the one I had seen. Mr.

St. Clair thought that a vigilance committee to deal with such matters should be formed. To accomplish this, and arouse public opinion he wrote out a description of the play, had it printed and distributed to some ministers, male school teachers and other citizens whom he thought might be interested. The Morality Department of the Police Force, whose duty it was to supervise these shows, had Mr. St. Clair arrested for publishing and circulating indecent and obscene literature. Great idignation was aroused. It was felt that even if action against Mr. St. Clair were justified, he should have been summoned to court and not subjected to the humiliation of arrest and detention in a cell in one of the police stations over night. Dr. T. Albert Moore, Secretary of the Board of Social Service and Evangelism of the Methodist Church; Dr. Shearer, Secretary of the corresponding board of the Presbyterian Church; Mr. W. E. Raney, K.C., who later became Attorney-General in the Farmer Government and then a Judge, Controller McCarthy and myself formed ourselves into a committee to defend St. Clair. The Criminal Code made it an offence to publish or circulate any obscene or indecent matter, but provided that it would be a valid defence, if the defendant showed that the public interest was served.

Mr. St. Clair admitted he published and circulated the document, that it was indecent and obscene because it described a show that in the document itself he characterized as indecent and obscene. He claimed, however, that the limited and carefully selected circulation he gave it was in the public interest, and necessary to arouse public opinion. The Crown urged that if he thought the play improper he should have gone to the police. The defence answered that in two ways, first by showing that an officer of the morality department had seen the show and had allowed it to continue. Then Mr. Raney (who was St. Clair's counsel), called me to the witness stand. He had me relate my experience and brought out the facts that I had done precisely what the Crown contended St. Clair should have done, with the result that the theatre paid a ten dollar fine and received a thousand dollars worth of free advertising.

Judge Denton, a very worthy citizen, and a good judge tried the case. He found on the evidence that St. Clair's document was a true and unexaggerated account of what occurred in the Star Theatre that day. He also found that the document (and hence the show) was indecent and obscene. He found, however, that Mr. St. Clair was not justified in printing such a document. He stated his entire confidence in the good intention of the accused but was of the opinion he was trying to do a good thing in a wrong way. He therefore found him guilty of the charge but stated he would suspend sentence, if St. Clair would give his own personal bond, not to offend in similar fashion again. On the advice of the committee he refused to sign any such bond. The Judge was most uncomfortable. It was evident that his sympathies were wholly with St. Clair and that he was disgusted with the action of the police. Very reluctantly he imposed a fine of twenty-five dollars or ten days in jail. St. Clair again on our advice refused to pay the fine. He was quite willing to spend the ten days in jail for the cause. If they had put him in jail we would have organized such a demonstration on his release that would have shaken the city. The authorities fearing such a result simply did nothing. That fine has never been paid to this day, and St. Clair was not sent to jail.

Following this a group of ministers and laymen got together and organized a great protest meeting in Massey Hall, Toronto's largest auditorium at that time. The Hall was crowded with a good representative audience. Prominent citizens gave addresses and a series of resolutions was passed. One of the resolutions named a committee of forty who were requested to carry on a campaign to clean up the theatres of the city. This committee was carefully chosen.

It consisted of prominent business and professional men and ministers. Mr. James Ryrie was elected chairman and I was appointed secretary. With the consent of my church board, a retired minister was engaged to relieve me of some of my pastoral duties, that I might have time to give to this work. During a period of two years, I either saw every stage show that came to Toronto or had a report on it by some reliable person who had seen it. Our friends were fond of calling us "The Forty Thieves."

One of the first results of the agitation was the appointment by the Toronto Board of Police Commissioners of a censor and an assistant censor of plays and theatres in Toronto. The cases in court had demonstrated that the supervision by police officers was a failure. The average policeman possessed neither the literary knowledge nor the understanding to do such work. The pay given to a policeman was not sufficient to command the services of men competent for such a task. The two men appointed were experienced newspaper men. The assistant censor had been dramatic critic for one of Toronto's daily papers for some time. They both understood the theatre. They were also men of fine personal character. Their task was far from being an easy one. There were many of Toronto's citizens who resented any interference and would have allowed theatres to put on any show that would attract enough supporters to make it a paying venture. At the other extreme were those who were opposed to the theatre altogether. If the censors had met their views, the theatres would all have been out of business in short order.

Between these extremes were two groups. The first were suspicious and fearful of censorship, not because they had any sympathy with indecency but because censorship had so often been the instrument of tyranny and the expression of prejudice.

There was still another group, who while they did not relish the idea of censorship, were convinced that call it what you will, some supervision of public places of amusement was necessary. As long as there were men of such low principle and selfish character, as to exploit for gain the weaknesses and passions of their fellowmen, some control must be exercised. They felt that as these places were licensed by the city, it was due to youth, especially those away from home, to make sure that they were at least decent.

For a time the censors were a bit over cautious and hesitated to make use of the legal powers at their disposal. They were both sworn in as police constables and could at any time have arrested any actor putting on an indecent act. However, they used methods of persuasion and after a short while most of the theatre managers learned to confer with them. The censors obtained from New York and other American cities advance information as to the character of plays proposed to be shown in Toronto. The managers were advised not to bring certain plays and if they showed a disposition to question the advice, were warned that prosecution of both manager and actors would follow the first performance.

During the time in which I acted as Secretary of the Committee of Forty I had an interesting and somewhat amusing experience. The Grand Opera House on Adelaide St. was the smallest of what were known as legitimate theatres in Toronto at that time. It was owned and operated by Mr. Ambrose Small, who some years after suddenly and mysteriously disappeared and was never heard of. There had never been any complaints as to the character of the plays staged at the Grand. One Monday morning my telephone rang.

"This is Cowan, manager of the Grand Theatre speaking. Mr. Coburn, Mr. Small, my employer, is very anxious to maintain a high standard for the Grand Theatre. We are anxious to retain the good will of the decent people of this city. There is coming to our theatre for this week a brand new play. Tonight is to be its premiere. I confess we are a little nervous about it and would like your opinion. If you could oblige us by coming to the theatre this morning we will have the company put on a full rehearsal and I promise you that anything you find to be objectionable will be eliminated."

I accepted his invitation but asked that the official censor be invited and also two or three of my committee of forty. From a moral standpoint little objection to the play could be made. I offered two or three suggestions which were cheerfully accepted by both the manager of the theatre and the company. Then the manager turned to me and said:

"Mr. Coburn, my employer and I are determined to keep this theatre clean and decent. But you know we cannot always be sure of everything that actors bring to our stage, we want your help. Two of the best seats in the house for each and every performance are at your disposal. We hope you will use them often; the oftener you do so, the better we will be pleased. We promise that what we have done in this case we will do in all others. Whenever you see anything which in your opinion is not proper in a public performance, please report to me at the close of the show, and I guarantee it will be eliminated."

It was highly amusing to many of my friends that a Methodist preacher was given such power in a theatre. I attended the Grand as often as I could find the time to do so. I found the manager as good as his word. On one occasion I went into his office and said:

"Mr. Cowan, there were one or two items in your show tonight I did not like. I would not say they are obscene, I do not think you could be convicted for them under the criminal code, but they were vulgar and a little bit suggestive. One thing I noticed. Near me there sat a nice, intelligent looking young couple, a boy and girl in their early twenties I would say. He might have been a clerk or a student, she might have been a stenographer or a clerk.

I sized them up as a pair of decent youngsters who had come
to your theatre for an evening's entertainment. When this
episode came on, as it proceeded I saw that this young lady
was embarrassed."

"Thank you, sir," said Mr. Cowan. "That is just the
kind of thing we want you to do for us. We have many
young people like the couple you mention. They come here
because they are not able to afford the higher prices of
the large theatres. We certainly don't want anything on
our stage that will embarrass any young lady. Those items
will not appear again."

As a result of the good work of the censors, Toronto for
many years had the reputation of having the cleanest stage
of any city of its size on the North American continent.
Unfortunately some years ago the City Council, as a matter
of economy, dispensed with this service, with very undesir-
able consequences.

3. *The Star Again*

In the St. Clair case, as shown in the preceding story,
the Judge found on the evidence that Mr. St. Clair's leaflet
contained a true and unexaggerated account of the play in
the Star Theatre and that the leaflet was indecent and
obscene. We then demanded that the Star be prosecuted for
putting on an indecent and obscene play. The request
could not well be denied. We also urged that the case be
transferred from the local county court to the Supreme
Court. By a Writ of *Certiorari* this was done. So in due
time the manager of the Star was arraigned before a judge
and jury of the Assize Court for the County of York. The
counsel for the defence was a very able lawyer and a colour-
ful character, T. Herbert Lennox, K.C. He was a member
of the Legislature, a most active politician and a great mixer.
It was said that he knew more men in the County of York
by their first name than anyone else. It was also said that

it was very difficult to convict any person in the County if Herb Lennox defended him. Herb would challenge enough jurymen to make sure that at least one or two of his friends were on the jury. These men would stand between Herb's client and a verdict of guilty. The worst that could happen to him would be a disagreement. He used this very method in the Star case. The evidence was quite clear. There was little dispute as to the facts. It was obvious that the show was a low, disgusting performance. Judge Middleton delivered a strong charge against the accused. When the jury filed in, to everyone's surprise they announced the following verdict and rider:

"It is with exceeding great difficulty that we bring in a verdict of not guilty, but the jurors wish the citizens to know that they feel that the proprietors and those in charge of show houses cannot be too strongly censured for allowing such plays as this, suggesting anything that is immoral, indecent or obscene."

Now, inasmuch as the charge against the theatre manager was one of putting on an indecent show, the verdict and rider were contradictory. When the verdict was announced all the spectators excepting myself, including the newspapermen, left the court. They evidently thought that all that would follow would be the formalities of recording the verdict and discharging the accused. But when these formalities had been completed, the Judge turned to that jury and gave them, the police and the theatre a severe castigation. He spoke as follows:

"I assume from the fact that you have taken so much trouble with this verdict that it is honestly and conscientiously arrived at. I may frankly say that I entirely disagree with it. I cannot see how any reasonable man could have any doubt that that play was anything else than immoral, indecent and obscene, and I cannot see how you found that even on the defendants' evidence you could arrive at any other verdict. The rider that you have added to your verdict indicates that you have some doubt, and while now it is my duty to discharge those accused, I hope they will recognize the fact that it may be difficult to find another jury that will take a similar view when a play of that kind is again produced. I hope that those in charge of the morality department of this city will not regard this verdict as in any way condoning the laxity that has prevailed; I do not think that we can be proud of the censorship that permits the production of a play so vile and unclean as this play. The Department of Justice has been brought into disrepute by this trial. The man who drew the attention of the public to this and who described what took place in the theatre in a way that seems to be substantially undisputed has been convicted of publishing obscene literature, while those who produced the play have been by the opinion of this jury acquitted. It is nevertheless my duty to direct that they should be discharged."

I saw at once that while we had lost a legal battle, if the story of that scene could only get proper publicity, we had won a moral victory. Fortunately the court reporter was a friend of mine—a comrade in a big temperance fight some years before. The difficulty was that he was a genuine Scotch Presbyterian, a sincere Sabbatarian, and it was nearly midnight on Saturday when the court rose. I had to have that story for the Monday morning papers. Could I get my friend to do the work on the Sabbath?

About nine o'clock Sunday morning I called him by telephone.

"Fred," I said, "I'm going to ask a great thing of you—something which you wouldn't do and which I wouldn't ask except under grave necessity."

"What is it? You know if it's something that I can do for you I'll be glad to do it."

"I know that Fred, but this involves a bit of work on the Lord's Day, and I know how averse you are to that. But it is necessary."

"Well you know, Mr. Coburn, that a work of necessity or mercy is all right on the Lord's Day. Our Lord himself taught us that."

"Fred, what did you think of that scene in court last night?"

"Think of it," he snorted, "think of it, need ye ask? In all my long experience in court, that positively caps the climax. For a jury to bring in a verdict of not guilty and then to turn around and in a rider imply that the accused had done the very thing with which he was charged, was unheard of, a disgrace to the City of Toronto and the County of York. But, oh man, didn't the Judge do fine? Aye that was a grand speech he made. He was good and mad and with good reason. I was talking to him in his room after. 'Fred Monteith,' says he, 'if I had the power, I would have sent every one of those cowardly jurymen to jail. It's a shocking thing when the administration of justice falls into such hands. Think of it Fred, twelve of them agreeing to a thing like that. If there had been only one decent man in the group, he could have held out for a disagreement. Well, I guess they know what I think of them.' Aye, and Mr. Coburn, I would have you know that the Judge is a good staunch Scotch Presbyterian."

"All right, Fred. For once I must admit that your Presbyterian did as well as any Methodist could have done—and that is some praise, don't you forget, Fred Monteith."

"Well, what's this thing you want me to do?"

"Fred, last night we lost a case but won a moral victory. It will be of no value unless it gets publicity. I want that jury's verdict, rider and all, and the Judge's reply, in Toronto papers tomorrow. I want six certified copies of the same furnished by the official court reporter. Needless to say, he will be paid—not on the Sabbath but in due time. I have strong faith Fred, that loyal Scotch Presbyterian though he is, said reporter will be so eager to further the cause of decency that he will regard this as a work of necessity. Now Fred, you know this official reporter pretty well, do you think he'll do it?"

"Do it, Mr. Coburn? I'm proud to be in a position to do such a job—even on the Sabbath."

I then called up Dr. Shearer, and Mr. W. E. Raney, K.C., and arranged a meeting for the early afternoon. The editor of Toronto's leading newspaper, *The Globe*, was the Rev. J. A. Macdonald, a sturdy and effective defender of all good causes. He wielded a mighty pen. Dr. Shearer said:

"You get the copies, Coburn, and I'll go and get Macdonald to put on his war paint. If you don't see something startling in tomorrow's *Globe*, I'm mistaken."

Sure enough—on the editorial page, in a box, was the jury's verdict and rider, and Judge Middleton's reply. Then immediately following was a scathing editorial in Macdonald's most trenchant style.

The foreman of the jury was a very respectable citizen, a prominent worker in a Methodist church. He explained that from the first, ten of the jurors were for conviction but two were obdurate in their opposition. They offered, if the accused was acquitted, to agree to any sort of rider the other ten desired to add. The foreman said the ten discussed the matter and finding themselves helpless to secure a conviction, came to the conclusion, that to do what they did was better than to have a disagreement—a trial without result. They believed that their rider would stir public indignation quite as much as a verdict of guilty. In this they were right, though how they could reconcile their verdict with their oaths is difficult to see. An interesting sequel was that the two jurymen who had refused to convict, as soon as the court opened on Monday morning asked to be excused from further duty as they had very pressing business matters. Herb Lennox had scored again.

12

SOCIAL WORK

1. *Prayer Meeting or Town Council*

"Hɪ ᴛʜᴇʀᴇ, hold on a minute, Mr. Coburn."

Going down street one morning in the town in which I lived, I was accosted thus by one of my fellow citizens. When I heard my name, of course, I stopped and waited until the man caught up with me.

"Say, Mr. Coburn, have you heard what's going on in this town today?"

"I can't say I have. You're the first person outside my family to whom I have spoken. What's up?"

"Plenty. You know Murray Carter and Bill Peters. Well they were on quite a spree night before last. Shortly before midnight they came tearing into town in a motor car, hooting and yelling like madmen. They tore up one street and down another and acted like rowdies. Well you know our Chief of Police, how decent and faithful to his duty he is. First thing yesterday morning he went to the magistrate and laid an information against these men. They are to be summoned to police court and dealt with as common drunks."

"Well isn't that what they were that night? Why shouldn't the Chief enforce the law?" I replied.

"That's just what I say, but some folks in this town don't think so. You know these two men are among our top notch citizens. Murray, as you know, was a Member of Parliament. If the Chief had found poor Joe Kelly in the ditch drunk, of course, everybody would say it was O.K. for him to run him into the lock-up. But these gents are different. I'm afraid there's going to be a fuss over it. I have it from Councillor Logan that a canvass is being made of the Town Council to get the Chief dismissed."

"The Chief dismissed, and for doing his duty? Surely not, I can't believe it!"

"Well sir, it's on the go, I tell you. Logan himself is solidly behind the Chief and he says there is one other member of the Council who he is sure will stand by him. But he says the other four members are doubtful. You see, Mr. Coburn, it is hard to get real good men to run for the Council. They say it takes too much time from their business, but don't you think it is the business of good men to see that the town is run right?"

"Of course I do, Joe. The lack of a sense of social responsibility on the part of so many decent, intelligent citizens is one of our perils. It is one of the weaknesses of democracy."

"Yes, that's what I think, and often men of low intelligence and weak character get into office. Then when an issue like this comes up, see where we are?"

"What can we do about it?"

"Well Joe, I promise you this, that if our Chief is dismissed for doing his duty, there'll be the jolliest row this town ever saw. But if the proper steps are taken, I think such a disgraceful thing can be prevented."

"Oh, I'm glad to hear you say that, sir. If I hadn't seen you on the street, I was coming up to the parsonage to tell you."

"Thank you, Joe, glad you told me. I'll get busy at once."

After a little careful inquiry I found that my friend Joe was no alarmist or purveyor of fairy stories. Some of the most reliable men in town were alarmed. They told me frankly they were not at all sure that the Town Council, as constituted, would sustain the Chief.

The more I thought about the situation, the more serious it appeared. Carter and Peters were men of wealth and prominence in the community. One of them was a regular attendant at my church services and one of our largest contributors. Bill was always very friendly and courteous in his relations with me. He was not really such a bad man, but weak, and completely under the influence of the other man. If the Chief were dismissed what a blow it would be to law and order, and what a lowering of the moral standards of the town; what an object lesson to the youth of the place. No, it must not be. Apart from the injustice inflicted on a faithful officer, it would be a calamity for the town.

I found a meeting of the Council had been called for the evening of the following day, presumably to deal with the matter. That was prayer meeting night in my church. I told some of my women they would have to run the prayer meeting as I was going to the Town Council meeting. I got together a group of good men representing various churches and we went in a body to the Town Hall, marched in and sat down in the front row of seats. It was interesting to watch the faces of the members of Council. Logan and his friends were all smiles but some of the other men were quite uneasy. There was little business to be done but they dragged it out as long as possible. We had come there that night on business, and were prepared to stay with it until morning, if necessary. Finally all business was completed, and we expected the motion to be made to dismiss the Chief. But no such motion was ever made at the Council board. The Mayor asked: "Has any member any further business to bring before this Council?"

There was a long pause, finally one of the four men of

whose attitude we were doubtful, said: "Mr. Mayor, I move that this Council do now adjourn."

The motion was seconded by Logan, put to the meeting and carried. In the presence of that little group of determined Christian men, no member of Council had the courage to make the motion dismissing the Chief.

The great majority of the citizens were delighted as the Chief was very popular with all but the law-breakers. I found, however, that some of the saints (?) in my church were inclined to question my conduct in deserting the prayer meeting for the Council Chamber. They would have had me join in singing about the "Sweet Bye and Bye" regardless of the unsavoury "Now and Now" that was being promoted. The following Sunday from the pulpit, I told these folks and all others who came to church, that religion was not meant for Sunday and the church alone, but for the home, the market place, the halls of legislature and the Town Council.

2. *A Man With Eighteen Children*

One of the most delightful holidays I ever enjoyed was at a Georgian Bay summer resort in 1928. On a Sunday morning I conducted a service under the auspices of the local Tourist Association. The announcements were made by the treasurer of the Tourist Association, a well-known business man from Toronto. He made a fervent appeal for a family whose house had been burned and who were living in a stable. He thought there were about twenty of them. They were very poor, he said. He stated he had used $25.00 of the Association's funds to buy some groceries for them. He urged that if any persons had any surplus clothing, they donate it for the use of these poor people. After the service he told me the people were French Roman Catholics. I asked if the priest had been approached. He replied that he understood that had been done, but with little result. I pointed out to him that $25.00 worth of groceries could not last twenty people very long, and further, that any clothing the tourists would give, would probably be light summer things that would be of little use after a few weeks. I suggested too, that some effort be made to solve the problem. It turned out that the youngest child was only one year old—the others of various ages up to about 18. So it was arranged that two of us should visit the house and get all the facts. In the meantime one of the storekeepers gave me some information about Jim Tremblay.

"He is as decent a man as I know," he said. "I have some timbered land. If Jim were to buy any timber from me, I would accept his statement as to the quantity taken without question—and that's more than I would do with most of the men around here. Jim is as honest as the sun. He has worked hard all his life. He didn't spend his money in drink either, but used it to support his wife and large family. A few weeks ago his wife died leaving him with all these children to care for. I'll tell you something about that, that will show you what kind of a fellow Jim is. When his wife died, a few of us boys who knew him clubbed together and sent to Midland for a coffin. We told him it was a present from a few of his friends. Shortly after the funeral I engaged him to repair the government dock of which I have charge. The price was $25.00. Jim came into my store and bought $15.00 worth of groceries. I offered him the balance of $10.00 in cash. 'No,' he said, 'let that go on the cost of the coffin.'

" 'Oh, but Jim,' I said, 'we told you that was a present from your friends. You don't owe anything on that. Here take your money.'

" 'No, Mr. Fraser,' said Jim, 'I could not do dat.'

" 'What?' said I.

" 'Let other men pay for my wife's coffin. I must do dat myself.'

"I could not help feeling a great respect for this uneducated man who showed such a spirit of independence and of reverence for his wife's memory," Fraser continued. "I finally compromised with him by giving him $5.00 and allowing $5.00 to stand on the coffin account."

With this information in mind, and in company with one of the tourists I visited Jim's home. Sure enough it was a stable, but the situation was not quite as bad as that would seem. The building had been built for a stable, but had not been actually used as such. Jim had thirteen children under his care. After his wife's death he had persuaded a couple, relatives of his wife's, to come and keep house. These people had four small children of their own. That made a total of twenty — three adults and seventeen children under one roof. Jim received us with great friendliness, and at once we proceeded to business. He told me his story in substance as follows: "My older brother, he marry young, have tree children, then his woman die. Then he marry another woman, she have five more children. Then my brother he drown, leaving wife and eight children. She poor, no money. We people poor. My father poor, no able to help much. I say I must tak care of my brother's wife and children. What kind of brother would I be if I let them starve? I think hard. How can I do it? The woman say she and children come and live with me, or I come and live with them. I say, 'No, I will not have scandal about my brother's wife,' so I say to her, 'Marie, we go to the priest and marry. Dat is the only way.' She say, 'So soon?' I say, 'What we wait for?' These children cannot wait for food. This is my duty to my brother. We have no marriage love? Maybe not—maybe dat will come some day. Anyway we do our duty. So we went to the priest and he marry us all right."

The records show that every year after that, but one, Jim and his wife were blessed with another little French Canadian. When Jim told me the story, I pointed out that there was one year in which no child came. "Why was that Jim?" I asked. With the greatest gravity, Jim replied: "Oh I can explain dat. My wife take sick, she have ammonia on the lungs. Baby come too soon and die. Too bad, too bad, nice little fellow but so small he die. She nearly die too, very sick, dat ammonia bad stuff on the lungs. She and I have ten children and if she hadn't taken sick and died last spring, we would have had another. She leave me with ten of ours and three of my brother's to care for. Two of my brother's children are married, three of them have gone to work for themselves, so I have thirteen here to get food and clothes for."

Then Jim proceeded to explain that his greatest anxiety was for the oldest girl—fifteen years old. "She is a good girl," he said, "but she is nearly a woman and knows so little dat she needs to know. So I arrange with a nice woman from Buffalo to tak her to her home. This woman and her family come up here many years. I know them well. They are fine people. She, the woman, agree to tak my girl home and let her work for her and she teach her the tings a woman should know. But when I tell the priest, he get vera cross. He say: 'You do wrong Jim Tremblay. You should keep dat girl at home to keep house for you and the rest.' But I am afraid. I have to go away to work. There are bad young devils in this country. My girl is not bad but she doesn't know. What might happen when I am away, I do not know. But the priest he will not listen at all. He say, 'No, no, keep her home'."

Then looking at me very earnestly, Jim said, "What you tink, am I wrong or right?" I said, "Jim, if that priest had in his home as many children as you have had, even as many as I have had in my home, he would know better. You are quite right Jim, and the priest is wrong." He reached out his hand and grasped mine, giving it a powerful shake. "Tank you, tank you," he said.

"You have been to the priest then, Jim?" I said.

"Yes, I saw him but got no help, he tell me he tak the ten smallest children if I pay $10 a month for each one. But I couldn't do dat, dat would cost a hundred dollars, and Meester, I never mak more than sixty. Sometimes only fifty-five and sometimes only fifty. I work hard but wages not high for man lak me, and so dat is all I can get."

I asked Jim when the priest would be in the neighbourhood again.

"Next Sunday morning," he said.

"Now Jim," I said, "if you do what I tell you, I think you will get somewhere."

"Oh tank you, tank you, sir, I will do whatever you say."

"Jim," I continued, "I have no desire to interfere with your church, or with this priest and his flock, but I am not going to allow a decent fellow like you and your children to suffer in this way, if I can help it. You need help, and you are going to get it if I can manage it. Now, next Sunday you go to this priest. Tell him again about the fix you are in. Then tell him that a Protestant minister has been to see you and that he has offered to take your ten youngest children and provide them with good homes, allowing you to pay what you are able toward their support."

Jim leaped to his feet and began to shout and dance and wave his arms. "Is dat so? You will do dat, eh? Sure ting?"

I assured him I would, though to tell the truth I did not know what in the world I would do with the brood if my offer were accepted. I was reasonably sure, though, that I would not be called on. I could not imagine a Catholic priest allowing a Protestant minister to get hold of ten Catholic children. Jim grasped my hand and shook it again until my arm ached, pouring out a volume of words—some French, some broken English, expressing his joy and gratitude.

Sunday afternoon a canoe was seen nearing our shore.

The lone passenger was sending it forward with mighty sweeps of his paddle. When I saw that it was my friend Jim, I went down to the dock. He leaped from the canoe, rushed up to me and grabbed my hand in both of his.

"Oh, tank God, you are a life saver. Say boss, I never saw such a change in a man. Dat priest, oh my! When I see him first, he not seem to care a bit. This time I tell him about you he get good and mad. 'Who is that man?' he say. I tell him his name is Reverend John Coburn from Toronto. 'Oh,' he say, 'I hear of dat fella. Well Jim, you go back and tell him to mind his own business. The Catholic Church can take care of its children, without any help from a Protestant preacher. And Jim, we take all your ten children. The boys will go to a boy's orphanage and the girls to a girl's orphanage and you pay what you can. You get them ready!' he say, 'queek, queek.'

"Oh," said Jim, gesticulating wildly, "you never see such a change in a man, tank you, tank you."

I was almost as well pleased as was Jim. The result was just what I expected and hoped for. One difficulty, however, remained. The children had so little clothing that they could not be sent on the journey without substantial additions to their wardrobes. Poor Jim had no money to buy clothes. The Tourist Association came to the rescue. The men gladly chipped in and furnished the money to buy the necessary materials. The women organized a sewing bee, and soon had appropriate garments ready and the children were started on their way.

13

AN EPISODE IN THE CHURCH UNION CONTROVERSY

It has been assumed by many that there was no anti-union sentiment in the Methodist Church. In this they are mistaken. There were many ministers and members of that church who had grave doubts and misgivings about the project. Two things saved Methodism from the strife experienced by the Presbyterians. First, the anti-union sentiment in the Methodist Church lacked adequate leadership. It was not organized. Secondly, Methodist people had been trained to accept decisions of the courts of their Church, especially when endorsed by a majority of the members. In harmony with the agreed on basis of union, the members of each congregation in each of the three communions was to take a vote by ballot on the question. This was done throughout Methodism in 1912.

Rev. George Washington, a retired minister, was one of the most sincere and saintly of men. With all his heart he believed in and loved the Methodist Church. While most kindly in his attitude to the people of other faiths, Georgie, as his brethren affectionately called him, was quite convinced that the Methodist Church was the most effective representation of Christianity in the world. He was greatly disturbed by this union movement. He feared that in the new church some of the evangelistic fervour characteristic of Methodism and the zeal in combating social evils would be lost or at least seriously modified.

The Conference of 1911 had sent to the Lemonville circuit (about 30 miles from Toronto) a newly ordained minister, Rev. W. R. Clements. While a student at Victoria College, Mr. Clements had done some downtown mission work under my direction. I had come to esteem him very highly and we became very close friends. A few weeks before the vote on union was to be taken in his congregations, he wrote me asking for advice and help. Lemonville was a four-point field. The minister could conduct service in only three of these churches each Sunday. (It was in the horse and buggy days.) The church board had engaged Mr. Washington, who lived in an adjoining town, to come out and take one of these services each Sunday. He had a horse and buggy, and had announced that he intended visiting every Methodist family within a radius of fifteen miles from his home, with a view of persuading them to vote against union.

"You know Mr. Washington well," Mr. Clements wrote, "what a saintly man he is and how tremendously in earnest he is about this matter. The people all love him and I am afraid he will do a lot of harm to the cause. He is one of the fathers in Israel and I am a mere boy. What can I do?"

Clements then went on to say that he and a few of his leading men had talked it over and had come to the conclusion that the best plan was to have a public debate on the subject, let the people hear both sides and then act as they saw fit. He suggested holding meetings in the two most central churches on the same day, one in the afternoon and one in the evening. He had spoken to Mr. Washington who heartily approved of the plan and readily agreed to uphold the anti cause.

"Now," said Clements, "I want you, if you will, to come

and uphold the cause of Union." It was quite a novel idea and I could see where I could get a lot of fun out of it.

We had two fine congregations that day. It was arranged that, as the one proposing change, I should open the discussion by a half-hour address. Mr. Washington would follow with a half-hour, then I would speak for another half hour and he the same. Then as I had to open the discussion I was to have 10 minutes in final reply.

In my first address I followed an old debating device, namely, I sought to put my opponent on the defensive. I told the people that this basis of Union that had been agreed on, practically unanimously, by the leaders of these three churches was an amazing phenomenon, and that like all phenomena it called for an explanation.

Things like that do not just happen. What causes produced it? I then related how the veteran leaders of these churches, not the young inexperienced novices, but veterans who had fought each other on many a well fought ecclesiastical battlefield, had met to "Explore the Possibility of Union." That was the exact phrase used. Some of them afterwards confessed that when they met they didn't think the possibilities were very bright. High mountains of difficulty loomed up. But here is what happened. First these men testified to a delightful spirit of Christian fellowship that pervaded the meetings. Then they all were conscious of a strange Presence in their midst. Finally as they discussed matters of doctrine, church government and administration from day to day, to their utter amazement the mountains of difficulty disappeared. Almost before they themselves were aware of it they found themselves at one. This wonderful document was the product of that meeting and the result of that experience. I argued that it called for an explanation. I then stated that I would give what I believed to be the true explanation.

"These men," I said, "found themselves at one, because One Master Mind was in control. The strange Presence that they felt was that of the Spirit of God. Under His influence they were led to see how insignificant and unimportant were the matters on which these bodies of Christians differed, and how tremendously vital were the things on which they agreed. "Now then," I continued, "if that explanation is the correct one, our debate ends right here. If this movement is of God, I am sure our good friend Mr. Washington would be the last man in Canada to oppose it. Of course, he may say I am all wrong, that that is not the correct interpretation at all. Very well, but I point out that if he rejects this interpretation, he must furnish us with another, and with one that will be adequate. It will not do for him simply to deny the correctness of my explanation. He must advance something that will satisfy the reason and conscience of Christian people."

In his first reply Mr. Washington ignored my challenge. His main attack on Church Union was from the theological standpoint. He read from the section of the Basis the following: "We believe that the eternal, wise, holy and loving purpose of God so embraces all events, that while the freedom of man is not taken away, nor is God the author of sin, yet in His providence He makes all things work together in the fulfillment of His sovereign design and the manifestation of His Glory." This, he claimed, was unadulterated Calvinism. It meant that Methodism would surrender its great doctrine of the free saving grace of God in Christ offered to all men.

In my second address I pointed out that Mr. Washington had ignored my challenge to account for the Basis. I urged that the question I had asked would not down. I then said that if in his second speech Mr. Washington did not give some answer to that question, I would ask the audience to believe that he had no answer to give.

On the theological issue I had a bit of real fun with my good old friend: "Mr. Washington has read to you a section of the Basis which he claims to be Calvinistic. I am

going to read it again, then I am going to read a few verses
from the first chapter of the epistle to the Ephesians. Please
pay the closest attention to both these passages. After reading from the Basis, I read the following from Ephesians:
"According as he hath chosen us in Him before the Foundation of the world, that we should be holy and without blame
before Him in love, having predestinated us into the adop-
tion of children by Jesus Christ to himself according to the
good pleasure of His will."

"Now don't you see how similar these passages are? I
submit that the same method of interpretation that finds
Calvinism in the Basis will find it in Ephesians. Friends I
confess I have suffered a great shock here today. As one of
the younger ministers of the Methodist Church I have
always looked up to Mr. Washington as one of the stalwarts
of Methodism. Other men might at times waver in their
loyalty to Methodist tradition and doctrine, but George
Washington never! Now to my amazement and apparently
unknown to himself, I find our good friend is at heart a
Calvinist."

Loud and prolonged laughter came at once from the
audience. To those who knew him the idea of George
Washington's being a Calvinist was just too funny for anything. Poor Mr. Washington! He was greatly surprised and
confused but he was too good a Christian to get angry.

In his second address, he attempted to answer my
challenge: "How did this basis of Union come to be? We
all know that the devil has great power" (Georgie had no
doubt whatever as to the existence of a real, live, personal
devil) "and the devil sometimes persuades good men to do
evil things. For instance he persuaded David to number
the people of Israel in defiance of God's command. This
is what I believe has happened in this case." Several of
the audience laughed.

In my brief summing up I said, "If the devil is running
the churches the sooner they are out of business the better.

But seriously, friends, I am sure you all feel with me that Mr. Washington has completely failed to answer the question. My explanation therefore stands. This Union is the work of God's Spirit. In that case your duty and mine is clear when the ballot is placed in our hands."

With some variations the performance of the afternoon was repeated at another church in the evening. The advantage of letting people hear both sides of a question and the strength of the Unionist cause were shown by the subsequent vote. On the whole circuit there was but one ballot cast against Union.

My father and mother had been ardent and life-long Methodists. They were at that time strongly and sincerely opposed to Union. The day before these debates took place I was at their home for dinner and told them of the programme for the following day. Mother looked at me sternly and delivered herself as follows: "John, you know how anxious your father and I are that wherever you go or whatever you do, you do well. But tomorrow I hope Mr. Washington takes the hide clean off you. I'd like to be there to applaud him while he does it. The idea of you, brought up a Methodist all your life, advocating the wiping out of the grand old Methodist Church and going over to the Presbyterians, that's what it means. This is one time you'll get no sympathy here, and no praying for your success will be done either."

In the Methodist Church there were thousands like my parents and my friend Washington. If a few determined men of similar spirit to the anti-union leaders of the Presbyterian Church had gone out, unfurling the banner of John Wesley and calling for loyal Methodists to rally round it, many would have responded. Fortunately no one did that. In the thirteen years between the vote in Methodist congregations and the consummation of the Union, some things happened that caused my parents and many others to modify their views. The bitter and unfair attacks made on Methodism by some anti-union leaders in the Presbyterian Church roused their resentment. Father passed on just two months before June 10, 1925, so that he had his wish often expressed, to die as he had lived, a Methodist. Mother lived for eleven years longer and cheerfully took her place in the new church.

14

HEROES OF FAITH AND ACTION

1. *John Dean of Mulmur*

JOHN DEAN was born in County Fermanagh, Ireland, in
1816. He was a real son of the Ould Sod. He came to
Canada in 1850 and to Mulmur Township, of which he was
one of the pioneers, in 1860. The land in Mulmur was
rough and hilly, some of it stony. It was thickly wooded
and before any crop could be had, trees had to be cut down,
sawed into logs, made into large piles and burned. Millions
of feet of fine timber, not only in Mulmur but throughout
Ontario had to be destroyed. To us it seems tragic but it
was unavoidable. A major task was the erection of a barn
to serve the double purpose, a shelter for the farm animals
and a place of storage for the crops. At the beginning, these
barns were often made of logs. The trees had to be cut
down, sawn into required lengths, mortised at each end,
hewn flat on two sides, then placed one on top of another
to the required height. The spaces between the logs were
chinked with plaster or if that was not available, with mud.
With a substantial roof such a building was strong and
comfortable.

The placing of these heavy logs was a task requiring a

number of men, so invitations would be sent out for a barn raising and the men from the countryside would come. Some of them would bring a wife or daughter to assist the good lady of the house in serving the hungry workers with food. It was an important social event. In the sixties, whiskey was both plentiful and cheap in Mulmur. It had been the invariable custom at threshings, logging bees and barn raisings to have a plentiful supply of the "craythur" for the men.

About the turn of the century I was the anniversary guest preacher at the little Methodist Church at Whitfield. Of this church Mr. Dean was one of the founders and for over thirty years class leader. Though over four score years of age, with hair and beard as white as snow, he was still the recognized leader of this congregation. I was his guest for the day, and after a good supper while awaiting the hour of the evening service, at his fireside, he told me the story of how he raised the first barn in Mulmur without liquor.

"The gettin' of those logs ready for the raisin' was a big job," said he, "but finally it was done and we sent out the invitations. As the day of the raisin' drew near I was throubled about one thing—the whiskey. You see I had been converted at a Methodist revival meetin' and when I took the stand for Christ, I made up my mind to make a clean job of it. I had no use for these milk and water Christians. From the first, one thing was clear to me—that I should lave whiskey alone—and I have done so. Not a dhrop has passed my lips since my conversion. Then the question kept comin' up—how could I consistently hand out that stuff to my neighbours? I knew what it had done to many both in Ireland and Canada. I prayed a lot about it and talked it over with the missus. One night we sat up pretty late talkin' and decided to pray for guidance and the strength to do whatever was God's will. When we rose from our knees it seemed as clear as sunlight to me that there should be no liquor. So I says to my wife, says I, 'Lizzie dear, if we don't have any liquor, we'll be misundtherstood, we'll be branded as stingy skinflints, an' the affair will be gossipped about all over this part of the country. It won't be aisy or pleasant I can tell you. But if it is God's will, are you willin' to face it with me?' She just ran over, threw her arms around my neck and said, 'John dear, you know I will, an' if you felt it was your duty an' didn't do it, I'd be ashamed of ye.' I can't tell you, Misther Coburn, how that put strength an' courage into me. Putting me arm around her I said, 'Lizzie me darlin', with God and you on my side I'm afraid of nothin' and there'll be no whiskey at the raisin'.'"

"That was a pretty serious decision to make, Mr. Dean," I interjected. "How did you come out?"

"It was serious, more so than I expected. We had a fine day for the raisin', and a good crowd turned up. They all set to work with a will, the job was going fine. About ten o'clock my nearest neighbour, Tom Duffy, who was also one of my closest friends, came to me and sez:

" 'John, don't you think it's about time to pass the jug? The boys will work all the better if they have a good swig.'

" 'But there is no jug, Tom.' He just stared at me for a minute and then bust out:

" 'For marcy's sakes, you haven't gone and forgot that!'

" 'No Tom, I didn't forget it.' I then explained my position to him. It fairly staggered him.

" 'But John,' he sez, 'you can't do this. Everybody has whiskey at a barn raisin'. You can't go against the custom of the people like this.'

" 'Tom,' I replied, 'my Bible tells me not to be conformed to this world. What others do may be all right for them. I judge no man, but I must be guided by the Bible an' my own conscience, an' remember that same Bible says, "Woe to him who giveth his neighbour dhrink".'

"Tom shook his head, 'We've never had anything like this before. I'm afraid the boys won't like it!'

"He was right, they didn't. Soon the word went round that there was no whiskey. Not much was said, but most of the men picked up their tools and went home—some of them givin' me pretty black looks as they went. A few of the men stayed, but not enough to do the job. So no barn was raised that day. Some of the men thried to argue me out of it and persuade me to give in. One or two said they believed I was right.

" 'Men,' sez I, 'you all know what that stuff is doin' to some of our neighbours. There's one man, I needn't name him, as fine a fellow as stands in shoe leather, no better man in the township when he's sober, but you know if he gets a dhrink or two, he often goes on a spree for a week. He abuses his wife and children. More than once they had had to run to a neighbour's home in the middle of the night. Now men, that man was here today. Suppose the whiskey I gave him had started him off, and supposin' that he had gone home and struck his wife or a child, an' they had died as a result (and you know that might aisily happen), how would I feel? Then men, think of the young lads. There were boys here today, that I am sure never had a dhrink. Will I be the one to give them their first? Every drunkard in the world, got his first dhrink somewhere. What would I feel like if in after years, some poor drunken sot would stagger up to me and say "You gave me my first dhrink John Dean." No boys, with God's help the like of that will never rest on my conscience.'

" 'Well but John,' said one, 'what are you goin' to do? You can't run this farm without a barn, an' you can't get a barn up without the neighbours. You see for yourself what they think of it. It's all right to have principles, but we must be practical.'

" 'Jim,' sez I, 'I have given my life to God. I believe what I'm doin' is His Will. I know He'll not let me down. If I have to, I can sell this farm and maybe buy one that has a barn on it. If I can't do that, I can get some kind of a job in town. But one thing is certain, as long as I'm here, barn or no barn there'll be no dhrink. That's final.'

"Then Tom Duffy spoke: 'Well, John, you may be right or wrong, one thing is sure, you're a man, an' for my part I take off my hat to you. An' say John, don't do anything rash. I mean sellin' the place or anything like that. Maybe when the boys cool off a bit an' think it over, they'll change their minds.'

"About a week later, Tom came over one evenin' after supper. 'John,' he says, 'I've been talkin' to some of the boys. I met a bunch of them at the Post Office last night. I was able to make them see that it wasn't stinginess but because you were loyal to what you thought was right that made you do it. One of them declared that a fella who would stand up for his principles was a good kind of a man to have around. Some of them thought that you were a bit daft but really sincere. So John if you will set another day, I think we can rally enough to get up your barn. Some of the stubborn fellows may not come but there'll be enough I think.'

"I told him he could tell the boys, that while there would be no whiskey at the raisin', the missus and I would spend a bit of money and go to a little extra throuble to give them a good time. Well, Providence was kind and gave us another fine day. A fair crowd came, not as many as on the first day but enough to do the job. My wife and I kept our promise. Some of the boys declared it was the best barn raisin' they had ever been at. Then, Mr. Coburn, the next Sunday at church a little woman shook hands with me and said: 'Mr. Dean, I want to thank you. My Bob came home sober from your raisin'. Thank you and may God bless you.' That, sir, was worth all the throuble."

"I don't doubt, Mr. Dean," I said, "your action made an impression on the community."

"Aye, it seems it did. First one and then another did the same thing. None of them had any throuble. Oh, they

were chaffed a bit for belongin' to John Dean's teetotal gang.
Do you know, sir, that now, whiskey at a barn raisin', a
loggin' bee or a thrashin' is a rare thing. It seems to have
gone out of fashion in Mulmur anyway. An' of course, Mr.
Coburn, you know that a few years ago, the people carried
a Local Option law and closed up the last place in the township where the stuff was sold."

Mr. Dean lived to the ripe old age of ninety-four. He
was for twenty-seven years superintendent of the Sunday
School and for twenty-eight public school trustee at Whitfield. When he died in 1910 no man more fully possessed
the confidence of all the people and no one could be more
sincerely mourned.

About forty years after Mr. Dean told me this story, my
church honoured me by electing me President of the Toronto
Conference. One of my duties was to ordain the candidates
for the ministry. To my great delight I found that one of
the young men who knelt before me was James Homer
Dean, a great grandson of my old Mulmur friend. As I
laid my hands on his young head, I prayed, silently but
fervently, that to him would be given the same faith in God,
the same courage and the same unwavering loyalty to duty
as characterized his great-grandfather, John Dean, saint and
Mulmur pioneer.

2. *John Evoy of Bar River*

In 1877 John Evoy brought his family of seven children
and two grandchildren besides two daughters-in-law from
near Ottawa to the new, wild country of Algoma. It was a
great venture of faith and courage for a man of fifty-nine
years of age. The locality to which he came was almost solid
forest. There were no railroads or paved highways. One
government road ran from Sault Ste. Marie to Bruce Mines,
a distance of over forty miles, but it was very rough and at
certain seasons of the years almost impassable. The other

roads were little better than trails made by Indians and trappers through the bush.

Mr. Evoy brought his family and belongings from their old home to Prescott by wagon, thence by ferry to Oswego, New York, where he placed them on a sailing vessel bound for Sault Ste. Marie. This journey of close on a thousand miles through Lakes Ontario, Erie, St. Clair and Huron was made in three weeks. At the Soo, as it was called, he bought a small sail boat to which he transferred his family and goods, and sailed down the Ste. Marie River a distance of about twenty miles. He attempted to sail up a small stream emptying into the Ste. Marie, but found a sand bar blocking the way. The men of the party had to get out into the water and ease the boat with its precious cargo over the bar. Mr. Evoy named the stream Bar River, and such is its name today.

The house in which the Evoys lived for years was made of logs. For the first year it had neither doors nor windows. Heavy blankets covered the openings in cold weather and at night. Their only light at night was from homemade tallow candles, and the fire burning in the open fireplace. Grain had to be sown by hand, reaped by hand with a sickle or a cradle, and also threshed by hand with a flail. Nearly everything that the family ate or wore had to be produced on the farm. The nearest post-office was Garden River, about eighteen miles away. In winter the mail came to Garden River only once a week by dog team on the ice from Owen Sound, a hazardous journey, the round trip taking a week.

One of Mr. Evoy's grandsons told me that he remembers when a boy there had been a great influx of settlers into that part of Algoma and the merchants of the Soo and Garden River had failed to get in sufficient stocks. In February supplies ran out and there was no way of getting more until the ice broke up and the boats could run in the spring. For months they could get no flour, sugar, tea or meat. They lived on potatoes, game and boiled wheat grown on their own farm. He also recalls how one morning a big black bear stood on its hind legs, put its front paws in a window and looked in at the terrified boy at breakfast. The Evoys had a small pig, which when grown and fattened was intended to supply part of the family's meat for the winter. One day William's wife, who was alone in the house, heard piercing screams from the pig pen. Rushing out she saw a bear with the little pig in its forepaws running away. She seized a stick and took after the bear and pig. By brandishing the stick and shouting her loudest, she succeeded in frightening the bear so that he dropped the pig (none the worse) and scampered off into the bush.

One of the most serious features of the situation was the absence of medical services. Doctors were so few and so far away, over roads so rough that many suffered severely and died for lack of medical care. When little babies came to these homes in the wilderness, very few had the advantage of a doctor's attendance. Certain women in each community learned how to care for a mother and her babe under these circumstances. If the case was a normal one, these good women were usually successful, but if there was a condition requiring technical knowledge and skill they were helpless. In many such cases, before a doctor could be brought, both mother and baby were beyond help. These were the conditions faced by the Evoy family in 1877.

The reader may well ask why a man of his years would face such a difficult situation. He did it for his children and grandchildren. In Eastern Ontario he saw little prospect for them. In Algoma he secured three hundred and twenty acres as a free grant from the Crown. A year previous he had sent his oldest son William, to survey the land, choose a location and make what preparations he could for the coming of the family. William chose wisely, for the land he selected is now one of the finest pieces of farm land to be found anywhere.

John had had few educational opportunities but he made the most of them. If psychological tests had been in vogue in those days, his I.Q. would have been a high one. He was a man of great versatility. While his chief work of course, was that of a farmer, he was handy with carpenter's tools. He could shoe a horse and make a pair of shoes for a man. He often did all these things, having with commendable forethought brought the necessary tools with him. He knew that some members of his large family would suffer from toothache and that in the new land no dentists were available, so he brought with him a pair of forceps. If any case of toothache failed to yield to the home remedies applied, the forceps without benefit of anesthetic, simply removed the offending tooth. As it became known in other settlements that Mr. Evoy could pull teeth, people came to him for that purpose from considerable distances. John Evoy was a strong man and when he got hold of a tooth with his forceps it had to come. The patient would have one awful moment of intense agony, but then it would all be over and blessed relief ensue.

By far the greatest service Mr. Evoy rendered, however, was in the realm of religion. He brought with him strong religious convictions and a clear and definite religious experience. He knew his Bible and loved the services of the church. But, at Bar River, he found himself in a place in which there was no church, no minister, no religious services of any kind. Many people in such circumstances have been too ready to accept the situation and allow themselves and their families to drift away from religion. Not so John Evoy. No matter how busy the family was, every day he conducted family worship in his own home. Then he invited his neighbours to come to his house on Sunday, not to make a social visit or to indulge in idle gossip, but to engage in the worship of God. Being licensed as a Methodist local preacher, he conducted services. Soon the people in other communities heard of these meetings, and sent urgent requests for him to visit them. So it came to pass, that in that area of Algoma, before there were any churches or ministers John Evoy had a circuit of his own. One would think that a man of his years who had worked hard all week on his farm would feel the need of his Sabbath rest. Perhaps he found rest in a change of work or, like another Pioneer, found his meat and drink in doing the will of his Father in Heaven. At any rate on Saturday night or early Sunday morning he would set out on foot or on horseback and visit two or three communities, holding service in the humble log home of some settler. He broke to these hungry souls the Bread of Life, rebuked sin, offered mercy and forgiveness to the penitent. He visited the sick, comforted the dying and the bereaved, and buried the dead. In some cases, as no undertaker or mortician was available, with his hammer and saw he made the rude coffin, and then as a true, but unordained minister, he conducted the funeral service. On several occasions young couples came to him to be married, but not having the legal authority he was compelled to decline. He rendered this service without thought of fee or reward, for the Glory of God and the good of man. When at last the Methodist Church sent her saddle bag missionaries into that district, some little groups to whom Mr. Evoy had preached, formed the nuclei of Methodist appointments, which in some cases are today flourishing churches. The results of this unselfish ministry cannot be estimated. One has only to compare the moral and social conditions and the religious life of the townships of Laird, MacDonald and Tarbutt with other areas in Canada which lacked such leadership in pioneer days, to be profoundly impressed by the marvellous results of the work of this servant of God.

As before stated, in 1877 the nearest post-office to Bar River was Garden River, an Indian Reserve, eighteen miles away. Some time after his arrival Mr. Evoy applied to the government at Ottawa to establish a post-office. This was

done and at his suggestion was named Bar River. It has
retained that name until the present. Mr. Evoy was
appointed Post Master, a position which he held as long as
he lived to the entire satisfaction both of the postal authorities, and the community, thus adding one more to the many
ways in which he served the people.

I came to know Mr. Evoy in 1897. Bar River was
within the bounds of Echo Bay circuit. The old man's hair
and beard as white as snow, gave him a patriarchal
appearance, but his eyes were youthful, his mind alert and
he was greatly interested in church, community and national
life. Though nearing the four score years, rain or shine, he
would be in his place in the church. He was a great inspiration to his young and inexperienced minister. Two things
I loved to hear him do. He was a good singer. For an old
man he had a remarkably strong, clear, musical voice. He
sang bass and as there was no choir, his singing added much
to the service. Then in the class meeting, which was held
at all Methodist churches in that day, his simple testimony
had the ring of sincerity and truth.

After an absence of three years I returned to Echo Bay
and Bar River for a brief visit. I found my dear old friend
was very ill. In fact, everybody believed him to be on his
death bed. As he had not been in attendance at his beloved
church for many weeks, it was arranged that I hold a service
in his house and administer Holy Communion. When I
left, his oldest son followed me out of the house.

"Mr. Coburn," he said, "there is a matter upon which
the family would like your advice. Father as you can see,
is very ill. He is suffering from gangrene in one of his feet.
It is slowly creeping up his leg and will finally kill him.
The doctors say there is no remedy. He suffers a great deal
of pain and the doctor says that will increase as the disease
progresses. He also says that if father were twenty years
younger he would amputate part of the leg as that alone
would halt the progress of the disease. But as father is now

eighty-three years of age, there is only one chance in a thousand he would survive the operation. It's an awful decision we have to make. To operate will probably mean sending him to his death, but not to operate means weeks, perhaps months, of suffering. What do you think we should do?"

After a few moments thought I said:

"William, you and I believe that if your father dies on the operating table, all will be well with him forever?"

"Yes, Mr. Coburn, if any man alive is ready to meet his Maker it is my father."

"Then sudden death will be sudden glory and an easy, painless death at that. The alternative is severe, prolonged suffering with death at the end. Can there be any doubt as to which is the kinder thing for him? And then William, if the dear old boy has even one chance in a thousand to live, why not give it to him? Without any hesitation, I tell you that if my own father were in a similar state, I would favour the operation."

"I believe you are right, and I feel sure father will say the same when the case is put to him in that way. We haven't told him yet. We wanted first to be sure in our own minds as to what is right."

The operation was performed and to the great surprise and delight of the doctors, the family and many others, he survived. In a surprisingly short time, he regained his strength and insisted on being taken to his carpenter's bench. There he made a wooden leg for himself and later on, a kind of wheel chair. He lived for two years and finally died of pneumonia. A sound constitution and clean living throughout the whole of his more than four score years had pulled him through. John Evoy hadn't poisoned his system with either alcohol or nicotine.

"Mark the perfect man, and behold the upright
for the end of that man is peace."

15

SAINTS WITH LIMITATIONS

1. *William McDonagh, the Irish Methodist Preacher*

ABOUT 1860 a young Irish man named William McDonagh, was ordained as a Methodist minister. He was a man of untiring energy, dauntless courage, and evangelistic zeal, with a passion for all that was good and a hatred for all that he regarded as evil. His educational advantages in that pioneer time were few, but he had made full use of them. Though he had never graduated from any college, Victoria University recognized his intellectual gifts and his diligence in study, by conferring on him the honorary degree of Doctor of Divinity. He had a wonderful sense of humour, and a way of using it to the discomfiture of those who challenged his ideas or methods. He had such a sharp tongue, and was so forthright in his speaking that in most of the churches which he served, the people at first would be shocked and almost horrified. However when they came to appreciate his downright sincerity, and when especially they felt the beat of his warm heart, all misgiving vanished. While he was a terror to evil doers and hypocrites, he

156

became a beloved pastor and friend to his own people. It was truly said of him, that when invited to go back to one of his old churches to preach, he would draw larger audiences than any other preacher could command.

I once had the privilege of close association with him for a week. Many were the tales he told me of the pioneer days and of his work. Of these the following must suffice:

"Early in my ministry," he said, "I was sent by the Conference to a small town in the province of Quebec. Owing to necessary repairs to the parsonage, my wife and I were entertained for a few days at the home of one of the church officials."

It is probable that McDonagh's reputation has preceded him, and so the good man thought it wise to prepare him for what he would meet. "Mr. McDonagh," said the man, "my mother has been dead for some years and my father makes his home with me. I want to warn you that though he is a good man, none better anywhere, he is a little peculiar. He is a Universalist. He does love to argue with people, especially ministers, about what he calls his blessed doctrine."

"Well sir, he'll not argue with me," was McDonagh's rejoinder.

"I'm very glad to hear you say that, sir. I don't accept my father's ideas at all, yet I dislike hearing anyone contradict him. I will be very happy if no argument arises between you."

Late in the evening the old man put in an appearance. He proved to be a New Englander, a typical Yankee, drawl and all. Immediately after introductions the old man challenged McDonagh to a dispute. In spite of repeated urging the latter declined. Then the old man asked him to give his opinion of his blessed doctrine. McDonagh said, "No, I'll not do that either."

"May I ask why?"

"If I gave you my honest opinion of Universalism, I'm afraid your opinion of me wouldn't be very good."

"Nonsense, nothing you would say would annoy me in the least. Come on now, please tell me what you think."

"Well, you can't say I didn't warn you. You've asked for it, and insisted on it, so here goes—but remember this is no argument. At your request I am giving my honest opinion about Universalism, and you agree not to get mad. Is that it?"

"Right sir, go ahead."

"Very well, the Good Book informs us that at the beginning, God created our first parents, and placed them in a beautiful garden. There were all manner of flowers, and fruits for them to enjoy—everything they needed. There was, however, one tree of whose fruit they were forbidden to eat. In the day they ate of the fruit of that tree, death and disaster would overtake them. Everything went well, for how long we don't know, perhaps for a few hundred years, when one morning there walked into the garden a Universalist preacher. That preacher told them that God's word was a lie, that death would not follow eating the forbidden fruit. Unfortunately they were foolish enough to listen to the blessed doctrine of this Universalist preacher, as too many have also done since, and as you know sir, all our miseries flow from that hour."

With a chuckle, telling me this story, McDonagh said: "I tell you John, never again during my three years in that place, did that old fellow bother me about his blessed doctrine."

Another tale he told me was of an experience on one of his country circuits early in his ministry. A few weeks after his arrival on this field, the good people at one of the appointments became alarmed by the vigour with which he attacked certain things in personal and community life. After consultation they sent one of the mildest mannered and most diplomatic men of the group, to expostulate with this wild Irishman. The man presented himself one morning at the parsonage door. His knock was responded to by McDonagh himself, who with a broad smile and outstretched hand said: "Good morning brother Dixon," (all good Methodists in those days called each other brother), "come in sir, you're welcome."

"I don't know," said Dixon timidly, "whether I'll be welcome or not when you know the business on which I've come."

"I tell you, sir," said McDonagh with great heartiness, and giving Dixon's hand a vigorous squeeze and shake that made him wince—"I tell you sir, you're as welcome as the flowers of May—I don't care on what business you've come. Now sit down and make yourself at home. I'll ask Mrs. McDonagh to make us a cup of tea. Now, now, it'll be no trouble at all and I'm sure after your long drive it'll do you good. Do you know what they say in Ireland? 'Anyone who has passed nine doors can drink a cup of tay!' Well, you've done more than that."

Poor Dixon was a bit embarrassed but he couldn't escape. He had to drink McDonagh's tea and partake of a generous snack supplied by the lady of the parsonage. He was in no hurry to get to the point, in fact he would gladly have avoided it altogether. So after conversation about various matters, McDonagh said: "Brother Dixon, when you came into this house you intimated that you had come on some special business. What's on your mind, man? Don't be afraid to tell me, whatever it is."

In a very quiet and apologetic way Dixon explained that they had had a little meeting of the leaders of Bethel appointment, and that the men were all anxious about their church's future. Many of the members resented McDonagh's excessive plain speaking. The leaders believed that, if things continued as at present, in six months the congregation would dwindle to almost nothing. They had, therefore, asked him to explain the situation to the minister and on their behalf request him to change his mode of preaching.

McDonagh sat silent for a few moments, then turned on the unfortunate Dixon with this demand: "Brother Dixon, have you ever done any preaching?"

"No sir, I never felt qualified to attempt any such thing."

"Did any of the other men who attended your little caucus, do any preaching?"

"Not that I know of, Brother McDonagh. No, I'm quite sure none of them have."

"Then how dare they presume to dictate to a servant of the Most High God as to what and how he will preach? No, Brother Dixon, go back to your friends and tell them that McDonagh will not change his mode of preaching. But I'll make this bargain with you. I'll keep on preaching in my own way and as I believe God gives me the message for six months. If at or before the end of that time, the result they predict comes to pass, I'll publicly acknowledge I've been wrong, I'll apologize to them and the congregation and I will then change my mode of preaching. If, however, the result they predict does not take place, if the work of the church prospers, then I demand that every one of them publicly apologize to me. Isn't that fair now, Dixon?"

Dixon had to admit that it was fair and agreed to report to his fellows. There is no reason to believe that on the following Sundays McDonagh's sermons were of any milder quality. But a strange thing happened. The congregations began to increase. In the Methodist phraseology of that day, a revival broke out. For four weeks McDonagh preached to a full church every week-night and on Sundays extra temporary seats had to be put in the aisles to accommodate the crowds. The people had at last come to understand the man. His intense earnestness, his Irish humour and warmth of spirit had won them. The incident of Dixon's visit to the parsonage and its cause were for-gotten—but not by McDonagh.

Six months from the day of that visit happened to fall
on a Sunday. Mr. McDonagh stood up in his pulpit and
to a packed church related the incident. "Now," he said,
"I've kept my part of the bargain. You must keep yours.
I want every man who was at that caucus, and who
demanded that I change my mode of preaching, to come
forward to the altar."

A group of shame-faced men paraded as ordered. They
could not do anything else. "Now then, brothers, if any of
you think I should change my mode of preaching let him
speak up like a man."

Of course no one spoke. After a few moments of a
silence that could be heard, McDonagh said:

"So you've changed your minds. Well, thank God for
that, there's little hope for a man who never changes his
mind."

Here one of the men broke in: "Brother McDonagh, we
were all wrong, we just didn't understand you. Now we
believe you are a man of God. You preach the truth to us.
Sometimes it's a bit hard to take. There isn't one of us
that you haven't made ashamed of himself. But we wouldn't
have you any different from what you are for anything. We
apologize to you and hope you will forgive us."

"Forgive ye—no men, that's not my prerogative. Some
One else must do that. Let's get down on our knees and
ask God to forgive us all for anything we've done amiss.
I need forgiveness as much as any of you. I know I'm hot-
headed and a bit free with my tongue. Let us pray."

The whole congregation got down on its knees. (That
was the proper procedure in a Methodist Church then—
no sitting up at prayer time. Only the most ungodly or care-
less would think of doing that). As McDonagh prayed there
came to all the sense of an unseen Presence that awed and
inspired them. When they arose, McDonagh with tears in
his eyes grasped the hand of each man at the altar. "God
bless you men and thank God for this day."

2. *Sandy Robertson, Always a Schoolmaster*

In the third quarter of the last century there came into the County of Simcoe, Ontario, a Scotsman named Alexander Robertson. The community was a pioneer one, the land being heavily wooded. The first settlers, after building log cabins for the accommodation of their families, set about the establishment of a school. By far the best educated person in the new community, Sandy, as he came to be known, was appointed school master. This position he occupied for many years. In fact he became a sort of adviser-general to the people for miles around. He made their wills, and in many cases wrote their letters for them.

Sandy had brought with him from Scotland strong religious convictions. In his native land he belonged to a group known as the Morrisonians. Hence, when the first Methodist saddle-bag itinerant made his way to this community, he found in the schoolmaster a willing and capable ally in the establishment of a Methodist "cause." Sandy was a zealous student of the Bible and, as he had fair gifts as a speaker, was made first an exhorter, and then a Local Preacher in the Methodist Church. For many years he faithfully performed this function. The number of ordained ministers in the new country was small. Sandy was one of that band of faithful, consecrated men, who without fee or reward, travelled (often on foot) through the forests of Ontario, conducting services in the new settlements. It was the work of these men that enabled pioneer Methodism, with limited resources, to serve the country and establish herself in almost every community. If an adequate account of the early social and religious life of Ontario is ever written, the work of the Methodist local preachers such as Sandy Robertson, must be given a prominent place.

Sandy was a most sincere and devoted Christian. He loved his Bible and his church. He held to his opinions, religious and political, with great tenacity. Any statement that could be verified from the Bible or the Toronto *Globe*, he would accept without question. All others were matters of doubt. One who lived in his home for a year bore this testimony: "I never saw Alexander Robertson in an ill humour nor have I ever heard him speak an unkind or uncharitable word of anyone."

After his retirement from the active work of teaching school, Sandy removed to an adjoining town, a place of about 1,000 inhabitants. There for nearly forty years he lived, giving practically his whole time to the work of the local Methodist Church. The Methodist circuit consisted of this little town and three rural churches. Sandy was the Recording Steward and held four or five other offices in the church. In fact he was the most influential person on the field. This continued until he was far past the three score and ten. And he was still the schoolmaster. For many years he had made decisions for others. Entirely unconscious of any egotism, he simply went on making them, and expected others to obey.

I was told of one occasion on which my immediate predecessor was reading the Scripture lesson at a Sunday morning service. In Sandy's opinion the preacher had mispronounced a word. From his pew he promptly spoke up correcting the preacher's error.

At a meeting of the official board at which I presided, Sandy read the minutes of a previous meeting. I called attention to an error in one item. "You know, Mr. Robertson, that was not the motion which passed the Board."

"Maybe not, but I tell you, sir, it's what ought to be," this with a stern look and a most determined nod of the head.

Of course, Sandy had known the men of that Board since they were boys—had taught and when necessary soundly thrashed several of them in school. If they didn't know enough to make a proper motion, he was still the schoolmaster and would make the necessary corrections. As for this young minister, it was simply intolerable to have him call in question the work of one who had ruled the church for so many years. The minutes as read would stand.

That left only one course open to me as chairman of the meeting. I took the book and ran my pen through the incorrect record and wrote a correct one. Then I asked the Board if the Minutes as amended would be adopted. The answer being in the affirmative, I signed them and handed the book back to Sandy saying, "Let this be understood, Mr. Recording Steward, that it is not what you, or I, or any other individual thinks should pass, but what actually does pass this Board, by a vote of its members that is to be recorded in this book. No other record will be accepted as long as I am in this chair."

Sandy was too intelligent and too well versed in matters of procedure to fail to recognize the soundness of that position. I had no more trouble on that score.

One point on which Sandy and I clashed sharply was that of a new parsonage. On arrival, I found the old house in a deplorable condition. The Medical Health Officer of the town, who was also a member of our church, pronounced it unfit for any family to live in. In these circumstances, I felt I would not be justified in exposing my wife and children to such conditions. I called a meeting of the officials of the whole circuit and laid the facts before them. I told them that if they could not, or did not desire to secure a proper home for their minister, I would be forced to send my family to Toronto where they would be cared for, that I would board somewhere for the conference year, at the end of which I would make way for someone else. I stated emphatically that I would not expose my wife and children to unsanitary conditions for any group of men on earth. That presentation touched their pride. So even against Sandy's determined opposition, the Church Board (for once asserting its independence) voted to sell the house and build a new one. A building committee was appointed and set to work without delay.

One day Sandy met me on the street.

"Is it true what I'm hearin'?"

"What is that, Mr. Robertson?"

"About the new hoose, I'm told you and that committee have plans oot for it."

"Yes, that is quite true. The plans are all ready, and in next week's paper we will advertise for tenders."

"And sir, I am also reliably informed you are actually planning to put a bathroom in the place."

"Why yes, of course we are."

"Now see here, young man, we'll no stand for such extravagance. It's only three miles to the lake, go out there and hae a bath if you want one."

However, the new parsonage, bathroom and all soon became a reality.

Another difficulty was the Sunday School. For over thirty years Sandy had been the superintendent. Shortly after my arrival two of the most progressive men of the church came to me and urged that there be a change in the superintendency. Sandy was in the habit of delivering quite a long speech after the teachers had finished their work. He had tenaciously retained his broad Scotch accent. Most of his teeth had gone. When he became enthusiastic, as he often did in public speaking, the children could understand little of what he said. Attendance had fallen off. In fact some parents had difficulty in securing the attendance of their children.

"You'll have to get us a new superintendent, Mr. Coburn, or the school will just dwindle to nothing," said one.

"Well, that can easily be arranged," I replied. "You know the superintendent is elected every year at the Annual Sunday School meeting. The minister must nominate two or more for the office and election is by ballot. I will look around and select one or two good men and will nominate them along with Robertson. The members will then have their opportunity."

"It would be better if you didn't nominate Robertson at all," said one of the delegation.

"Say! you are brave fellows," I countered. "That would put the whole responsibility on one person, on me, instead of on the whole group where it belongs. Besides, good old Sandy, with all his faults, is entitled to the courtesy of a nomination. Over thirty years ago he took this job when there was no one else to do it. Through all the years, he has spared neither time nor effort. He has given of his best. I quite agree that the time has come for him to step down but I insist that he be treated decently. I will, as I said, nominate him and one or two others capable of doing the work. If he is re-elected it will be because you fellows haven't backbone enough to do your duty. But men, is there not a way by which we can avoid hurting the old man? If he is voted out he will feel it keenly. Could we not get up a sort of valedictory, make him a present in recognition of his long service and do it in such a way as to suggest that that service was now terminating? I would be willing to suggest that he be made Honorary Superintendent for life."

"We did try something like that a couple of years ago," was the reply. "We had a party, made him a nice present, read an address of eulogy and thanks with a good strong hint that his years of fine service were now completed. Sandy was very grateful but evidently did not detect the hint at all. In his reply he said, 'By the grace of God I'll die in the hairness!' No, that won't do."

When the annual meeting drew near, I consulted a few of the most deeply interested people. I told them whom I proposed to nominate. They were all satisfied with my selection, and said they were sure the change would be made.

"But men," I said, "can't this be done in a kindly way? Could not two of you go to him, tell him we all love him and very greatly appreciate his work, but that we feel a man of seventy-five years should step aside and let younger men have a chance? Tell him we'll make him Honorary Superintendent for life. I would go to him myself," I continued, "but you know he and I have had a bit of a battle over the parsonage and I am afraid he would think I was getting back at him. But surely some of you know him well enough to do as I suggest."

All agreed it was desirable to have the matter carried through in that way but how could it be done?

"What you say about his blaming you applies to all of us," one of the group said. "He is a fine Christian, but is very self-willed. He has been allowed to run things so long, he will resent any intereference. Whoever ventured to approach him would be blamed for the whole thing."

"I don't see that we can do a thing," said another.

"What you suggest is all right, Mr. Coburn, but we know this old man better than you do. I think I am on as friendly terms with him as any man in the church but I wouldn't dare to speak to him about such a thing."

Another who had up to this time remained silent spoke up, "As I see it the interest of the school and our children are of more importance than the feelings of any individual, no matter how good he is. No man holds any office in the Methodist Church for life. We are a democratic people. That is why we have an annual election. If the election does not permit the people to choose among two or more men, then it's a farce. You, Mr. Coburn, have the responsibility of nominating. We appreciate your taking us into your confidence. You didn't have to do that. We all approve of your proposed nominations. The responsibility for the results will rest with the people."

I knew the men were right, and I seemed unable to avoid what I felt would be the sore wounding of a good man. The annual meeting was held on a stormy night so the attendance was small. I made the nominations as I intended and when the ballots were counted Sandy received only two votes. He was a stricken man. Poor old chap, it had evidently never entered his head that they would want anyone else but him for superintendent.

Next Sunday, his place in church, that of his wife, his married daughter and her family were vacant. We learned that they were all in attendance at both services in the Presbyterian Church. The leading man in the Presbyterian Church was one of the town's merchants. He and Sandy had worked together for the same firm years before and had been fast friends throughout the years. On Monday morning this man, Mr. Telfer, called into his office one of his clerks, George Marsden, who was a teacher in our Sunday School.

"George," said Mr. Telfer, "I know something has happened in your church. The Robertsons and the Masons were all in our church at both services yesterday. If you care to tell me, I think perhaps I can help."

In a few words, the young clerk told his employer about it. Mr. Telfer watched for Sandy, and, when he came into the store one day, invited him to his office.

"Mr. Robertson," he began, "you and I are very old friends. We understand each other well and can speak frankly without fear of being misunderstood. Isn't that so?"

"Yes, of course, Mr. Telfer. I look upon you as one of my very best friends. What's on your mind?"

"You and your good wife were in our church on Sunday. I was very glad to see you there in the morning. I confess I was a little surprised to see you there again at the evening service. Since then, I have heard rumours of some little trouble in the Methodist Church."

"Well, so you might say, but I'm making no complaint."

"And I am expressing no opinion as to what may have been done. That is none of my business but there is something that is my business and that of every Christian in this town. Mr. Robertson, to put it plainly, no man can change his church at seventy-five and be happy. There is no one in this town whom I would more gladly see in the Presbyterian Church than you, but it just won't do. Perhaps you do not fully realize, Mr. Robertson, that in a sense you belong to all the churches. We have taught our young people to look up to you as an exemplary Christian, a saint in fact. Now if these young people discover that you ran away from your church because you were not elected to an office, what effect will it have on them? It won't do, my friend. It would be a blow to religion in this town. Not only the Methodist Church but all the churches would suffer."

"Well, what would you hae me do?"

"Something that may be a bit hard, Mr. Robertson. My advice to you as a friend, is that you quietly slip back into your old place in the church, and go on as if nothing had happened. I understand that you still hold several offices in the church. There will be plenty of good work for you to do. You are getting pretty well on in years, you know. The work of the Sunday School is quite a burden. It is quite possible that your friends thought it was too heavy for you, and that the work should be done by a younger man. Do not assume that they meant any unkindness to you. I am sure they all recognize and are grateful for the thirty-odd years of faithful service you have given. That is a record to be proud of. No one can take it from you and I am sure no one would want to."

"Aye, maybe you're right, but it'll no be easy. Everything seems to have gone wrong since that young whippersnapper of a Coburn has come here. First he demanded a new hoose, now it seems he wants a new superintendent for the school. The worst is he seems to be able to swing the people in with him. It used to be that the Board would take my advice on things. What are we coming to anyway?"

With a smile and a kindly pat on the shoulder of the old man, Mr. Telfer said, "Well I wouldn't worry too much if I were you. No doubt it will be a bit of a cross for you to accept this situation, but you know how often you have preached the doctrine that the cross is a part of Christian living. This may be your cross. You will bear it manfully I know."

The two old friends shook hands, Sandy simply saying, "Weel, I'll think aboot it."

After Mr. Telfer had done this splendid bit of Christian work, there was another who exerted even more influence than he, that was Mrs. Robertson. She was a quiet, gracious little woman, but she had a mind and a will of her own. It was well that Sandy, who had a somewhat fiery temperament, had such a life partner, one so gentle in spirit and yet so clear in her perception of what was right and wise. Long experience had taught Sandy, that it was the part of wisdom to listen to what Mary had to say.

Knowing her man so well she did not act hastily. She waited for a propitious moment and then she spoke. "Alex," she said one evening as they sat by the fire, "I been thinking about the church. You and I haven't a great while longer here. We've been in the Methodist Church for many years, and got used to it. I don't know how I could ever get used to the Presbyterian ways, and I don't believe you could either. You know how you like to preach the gospel. As a local preacher in the Methodist Church, you are asked to do it quite often. You know there is no such thing at all in the Presbyterian Church. As Mr. Telfer said to you yesterday, you are getting on in years and there'll be plenty for you to do in the church without the school. That school is a big job for any man. I really believe that after all its a good thing for you to be free of it. So now Alex, suppose next Sunday, we just go back to our old place as if nothing had happened?"

"Aye wife, I've been thinking a bit aboot it mysel'. If

you feel that way I'll no drag you away from your church. I can go back all right. Maybe it's God's will anyway, and if so who am I to oppose it."

So next Sunday Sandy and his wife and their whole family were back in their places. There was in the church an old Irishman named Davy Morrison. He had a great sense of humour and was fond of a joke. He could put on a poker face while he perpetrated some mischief on anyone. A day or two after Sandy's return Davy met him on the street. "I say Mr. Robertson, a week ago Sunday neither you nor your missus were at church either morning or evening, were ye sick?"

The old rascal knew the facts well enough but he wanted to see what excuse Sandy would make.

"No we were no sick," Sandy replied, "I had never heard the new Presbyterian minister preach, so we went over on Sunday morning. To tell the truth I didna think much of it, but I thought it was no fair to judge a man by one sermon, so we went back again at night to see if he would do any better."

During the second winter of my pastorate in that town, the church had an extensive revival, no wildfire or excessive emotionalism but a real stirring of spiritual life in the church and in many outside its membership. Sandy himself was deeply moved. One night he arose in a testimony meeting, his old face aglow and said, "Aye mon, but there's a graund atmosphere here and I'm just drinking down great gulps of it."

The sexton of the church had died a few weeks previously and his widow and daughters continued to do the work. One night it was quite stormy and I told them to go on home with the rest of the folk, and I would put out the lights and lock up. I was just ready to go when I heard a noise at the door. A moment later Sandy's old grey head and long white beard appeared and he started down the aisle toward me. I could not imagine what brought him back at that hour. I walked down the aisle and met him. He stopped and fixing his eyes with great earnestness upon me he said: "Coburn, I've felt hard at ye for some of the things you've been doing. You've been getting the church into debt that I'm afraid it can never pay, but aye laddie" (and that word laddie had a sort of caress in the tone of his voice) "aye laddie, the Lord's been using ye graundly. Gie us yer haund, mon."

There at 10 o'clock at night old Sandy and I stood alone in the church shaking hands. I do not know whether there were tears in his eyes or not. I suspect there were, but there certainly were in mine. From that on Sandy was my friend and defender. At the Board meetings he would occasionally give me a sly dig, "Oh aye, the young ministers nowadays dinna think they need the advice of them that's older anymore." But if a real issue arose, he was at my side.

In the Methodist Church in those days, while a minister could remain four years in a place, each minister was stationed either on his old field, or a new one each year. Legally it was only a yearly appointment. It was the usual custom to pass a resolution at the February meeting of the Quarterly Official Board inviting the minister to return for another year, that is if his return was desired. If no such resolution was passed it was a broad hint that the minister might be well advised to move on. At one of these meetings after the revival referred to, the usual motion was made and unanimously passed. I said, "Well Brethren, I'm going to be frank with you. This circuit with the town church and three county appointments is a very heavy one. I find the long drives tax my strength. I would greatly like to have a place in which I would not need a horse. I could then give more time to study. I understand there are one or two openings of that kind in the conference and if the opportunity should come my way, I feel I should take it."

Then Sandy arose and facing me delivered himself as follows: "Meenister, I'm thinking this is where ye'll have to stay anither year. There's a wheen of young lambs that's come into the fold. They'll no be knowing the voice of a stranger. They'll be needing their own shepherd. So I'm thinking this is where ye ought to stay."

3. *God's Good Man*

Marie Corelli wrote a novel under this title, taking as her hero a Cardinal of the Roman Catholic Church. I have always felt that such a characterization would fit the Reverend Charles Langford. Mr. Langford, of Irish stock, was born and raised a sincere Roman Catholic. His family had high hopes he would enter the priesthood. Being in very modest circumstances it was necessary that Charles should earn the money to defray his college expenses. He qualified as a public school teacher, and in due time became the teacher in a "little red school house" in rural Ontario where a large section of the community were Methodists. During his stay there these people held a camp meeting.

These camp meetings were old Methodist institutions. In the pioneer days the country was sparsely settled, churches were far apart, religious services were few and ministers were forced to serve large areas. As a consequence many communities were reached only once or twice a month. The camp meeting was a device to make up for this lack. A suitable wood lot would be selected, the ground cleared of underbrush, fallen trees and other debris. A large platform would be erected. The people would come from a wide area. Two Sundays and the intervening week would be given wholly to religious services, at least three each day. A staff of ministers would conduct the meetings. Tents would be erected in which the people lived for the week. The services were of an intensely evangelistic character. In earnest, impassioned sermons the preachers denounced sin in every form, and offered deliverance and a hope of eternal life to all who accepted Christ. The woods rang with the joyous hymns and songs of the large congregations.

As a good Catholic, Charles would have hesitated to attend a service in a Methodist Church, but out in the bush, that was different. Indeed many in those days who would not go to church were "caught" by the camp meeting. So Charles was induced to attend a service. Its warmth and evident sincerity appealed to his honest heart. He went again and again. The simplicity of the services contrasted with those of his own church, conducted largely in a foreign tongue, made a deep impression. These people told him he had a right to approach God without the intervention of saint or priest.

One night when the invitation was given he joined the other "seekers" at the penitent bench. Something happened then that changed the whole current of his life. The Church of Rome lost a priest, and Methodism acquired a most devout and faithful minister. He served many charges, each one of which was immeasurably better because of his ministry. He was not a brilliant preacher but his untiring and unselfish pastoral work, his gentleness, kindly ways, combined with real strength and courage, endeared him to his people.

Charles was a life-long friend of my father and mother. He knew each of them before they knew each other. He was the means through which I met my wife, he gave me my licenses as "exhorter" and local preacher, asked me to preach my first sermon in his church, married us and baptized all our children.

Charles suffered severely for his break with the church of his fathers. Their priest forbade his family to have anything to do with him, warning them that as a heretic he was accursed and that they would suffer if they showed him any countenance. One sister, however, kept up a surreptitious correspondence with him. She informed him of the sudden death of a younger brother of whom he was very fond. He hurried home, and arrived just after the body had been lowered into the grave. He begged that the coffin be opened that he might be allowed a last look at the face of his brother. The priest declared that as the body had been committed to the earth it would be sacrilege to reopen the coffin. His request was therefore denied.

Charles was taken to the home of this sister, who was married, and lived opposite the old home. In the morning Charles, looking out of a window saw his father in the barn yard. He went over to him and holding out his hand said: "Father, won't you shake hands with me?" Charles afterwards told my father, that he saw the struggle in the old man's face between the father on the one hand, and the loyal and obedient son of the Church on the other. The Church won. Without saying a word the father turned away and with bowed head walked slowly to the house, entered and shut the door.

Many years after this, while still a bachelor, Charles lived in my father's home for the greater part of a year. The Christmas season was a sad and lonely one for him. He was so sensitive and so considerate of other people, that he refused to intrude on the family circle. He was greatly depressed all through the holiday season and we were all glad for his sake when it was over.

Mr. Langford was one of the most thoroughly honest and sincere men I ever knew. One could not imagine his doing a mean or unworthy thing. He was so extremely polite, and so much afraid of causing embarrassment to anyone, that he was constantly apologizing to people, "Excuse me, brother" and "Oh, sister, I beg your pardon" were often on his lips. He did this so often that his friends greatly enjoyed his eccentricity. Some occasions were really comical.

The girl that I afterwards married lived next door to our house while Mr. Langford was with us. All attended the little mission church of which Mr. Langford was the minister. My girl and I were very young but very much in love with each other. The church being about half a mile away, the walks to and from the various services offered fine opportunity for courtship. One night a committee was to meet after the prayer meeting. Before the service Mr. Langford said to me, "Now, John, I want you to stay for that committee meeting."

"But Mr. Langford, I am not a member of that committee."

"Oh yes you are, my boy."

"I don't think so."

Of course I didn't want to stay for any old committee meeting. I had a much pleasanter prospect. So at the conclusion of the service, when the preacher's back was turned, I snatched up my hat and bolted. Before I had quite caught up with the young lady in question, the church door opened and a stentorian voice called out, "John, John, come back here."

What was a young fellow to do? Mr. Langford was a true friend who would make any sacrifice for the comfort of another. To ignore his earnest appeal would have hurt him deeply. So very reluctantly I turned back. After the meeting was over, he and I came home together. When we had proceeded about half way Mr. Langford suddenly stopped and said: "John, did Miss Susie have to go home alone tonight?"

"Well, how do you think she went?" was the not too gracious reply.

"Of course, of course, how thoughtless of me. So sorry my boy! So sorry! You must forgive me and I'll never do the like again."

The following morning he went into the home next door and most humbly apologized to Miss Susie. In fact he apologized to her each time he met her for a week. "So sorry, Miss Susie."

A minister's wife told me that Mr. Langford called once

at her father's home when she was a young girl. While his hat and coat were being disposed of in the hall, he felt something brush against the back of his legs. Evidently thinking he had accidentally collided with someone he turned quickly and without waiting to see who or what it was politely bowed and said: "Beg pardon, brother." Then he discovered it was the family dog who responded by vigorous and friendly wagging of his tail.

Mr. Langford was extremely absent minded. I never knew him to leave the house without coming back two or three times for something he had forgotten. On one occasion my father asked, "Has Mr. Langford gone downtown?"

"He has gone out, but he'll be sure to come back. He has gone only once," my mother replied.

Charlie, as his friends called him, did not marry until in his late forties. In his young manhood he was engaged to a splendid girl who died. He seemed unable to find anyone to take her place. However, at last he secured a mate. He and his bride arrived at his parsonage from their honeymoon in the evening. A friend had presented them with a very beautiful lamp. Coal oil lamps were used in most houses then. It had some new device that evidently Charlie did not understand. He was determined however, to light it, which he did. Something went wrong and there was a small explosion which threatened to set the house on fire. Charlie rushed out to get some water. Under an eaves-trough there was a large bucket full of rain water, which Charlie quickly emptied out, carried the bucket to the pump, filled it with good well water, with which he proceeded to extinguish the fire.

Perhaps nothing illustrated better the simplicity and sincerity of his character than the way he met his death. He was attacked by cancer of the stomach, too far advanced when discovered for any curative treatment. He insisted on the doctor's telling him the absolute truth.

"Then doctor, you can do nothing, there is no hope of cure?"

The doctor reluctantly admitted as much.

"Then the sooner it's over the better. I'm ready to go. I don't want one thing done to prolong my life."

He quickly arranged all his business matters and then quietly waited the end. The taking of food caused him pain, so he ceased eating, taking only a little water to relieve his thirst.

"Why should I torture myself simply to live a few more days? My work is done."

EPILOGUE—THESE FIFTY YEARS

Synopsis of Golden Jubilee Sermon

Preached by REV. JOHN COBURN, D.D., in Carlton Street
United Church, Toronto, June 15, 1947

TEXT: "For it is God who worketh in you, both to will and
to do of his good pleasure." Philippians 2: 13.

Fifty years ago, on the morning of Sunday, June 13th,
in company with several other young men, I knelt at the
altar of this church and took upon me the vows of the
Christian ministry. I was ordained by the late Rev. Albert
Carman, D.D., General Superintendent of the Methodist
Church, assisted by the Rev. S. G. Stone, D.D., President
of the Toronto Conference, and other ministers. I do not
intend tonight to talk about myself. Fortunately I have
something far more important, and I hope more profitable
to the congregation, to talk about. I would like just to call
attention to the words of St. Paul in the text, and to point
out that whatever any man accomplishes in life, is the result
of the work in and through him of the power of God. I
know full well, that if it had not been for His guidance and
strength, I could have accomplished nothing in the great
work which I felt called upon to do, and on which I entered
fifty years ago.

The world of today is a very different one from that of

1897. It is a much smaller and more inter-dependent world. Then there were no automobiles, radios, moving pictures, aeroplanes or atomic bombs. During the half century, the discoveries of modern science have greatly increased the comforts of life. In the homes of today, there are many utensils which were entirely unknown and even unthought of then. For instance, in the city of Toronto, electric lighting was found only on the streets, in public buildings, places of business and the homes of the rich. The homes of the poor, and even most of those of the well-to-do, were lighted by gas or coal oil lamps. We often hear eloquent eulogies as to the accomplishments of so-called free enterprise. As a matter of fact, there is no such thing as free enterprise. In view of credit controls, trust combinations, cartels and other devices of a similar character, no one can claim that enterprise is free. What people mean by free enterprise, is really private enterprise, and that is often contrasted with public enterprise, ownership and operation.

The undeniable fact is that private enterprise had, over a long period of years, by prohibitive prices, denied to the vast majority of the citizens of Toronto, the comfort and convenience of electric lighting. The spirit of God, however, put an idea into the mind of a man named Adam Beck. He was the author of a great movement. I was a young pastor in the City of Toronto at the time, and had the privilege of attending the first public meeting called by Joseph Oliver, Mayor of Toronto, to discuss the question of Hydro Electric Power. For centuries the mighty torrent of Niagara had been pouring forth its tremendous volumes of water, capable of producing at low cost enormous quantities of electric energy. The Hydro Electric Commission under government and city control was organized and began its work. The enterprise succeeded beyond the dreams of its founders. Public ownership and operation through the Hydro, have placed electric lighting and many other comforts in the homes of the poorest citizens of this city, and also carried them to remote hamlets and to many farm homes.

Effective Children's Aid Societies, juvenile courts, probation officers, Big Brother and Big Sister organizations, Mothers' Allowances, laws protecting the child of unmarried parents, child welfare councils, have all come into existence during the past fifty years. On my first field after ordination, on a distant home mission field, I found a most distressing case of the abuse and neglect of two children by their own father. They were being brought up in ignorance, filth and immorality. I made an effort to rescue these poor children from this awful condition, but failed, because at that time there were no facilities for dealing with such a problem.

Fifty years ago there was no Workman's Compensation or Old Age Pension. If a man was injured at his work and his employer was humane, he might be fairly well taken care of but, in so many cases, corporations, which have no soul, were ruthless in dealing with their men. A workman might have a strong case against the Company. He might sue in court and obtain a judgment, but the employing corporation could appeal from one court to another, until the unfortunate workman's funds were exhausted, and he would finally lose. The Workman's Compensation law of this Province is not perfect, but it is a vast improvement on the conditions of fifty years ago.

Fifty years ago labour unions were few and comparatively weak. Most men worked for ten hours a day and for small pay. Such a thing as collective bargaining was unheard of and, except by a few, unthought of.

In the religious world there has also been substantial progress. We have today, I believe, a truer conception of God, and a more reasonable interpretation of the Bible than when I began my ministry. A few years before my ordination, a very learned professor was dismissed from his chair in Victoria College, because of alleged heretical teachings. That same teaching would scarcely cause a ripple today. In fact it is accepted by a very large section of the ministry of most Protestant churches. There is also, within the churches, a fuller understanding of the social implications of the Gospel. Fifty years ago the emphasis was upon personal salvation. That emphasis remains, but it is accompanied by another which recognizes that there is no such thing as an individual isolated from society, and that the Gospel has a message for the redemption of human society, as well as the salvation of individual souls.

There is less rivalry and much better co-operation among the churches of Canada than existed fifty years ago. Perhaps the outstanding demonstration of that is the formation of The United Church of Canada. It was about five years after my ordination that a fraternal delegation from the Presbyterian Church appeared before the General Conference of the Methodist Church in the city of Winnipeg. The Rev. Dr. Patrick, leader of that delegation, took his courage in his hands, and made a most radical proposition to the Methodist Church, namely, that committees be formed to explore the possibilities of church union. The General Conference accepted his challenge and of course the General Assembly of the Presbyterian Church could not refuse to honour the proposition made by its own representative. Other Protestant denominations were invited to join, but the invitation was accepted by the Congregationalists alone. The result of that exploration is The United Church of Canada.

There has also been formed a World Council of Churches including practically all the non-Roman churches of the world, and in Canada, the churches have formed the Canadian branch of that institution. Recent conversations between committees representing the Anglican and United Church with a view to closer co-operation and securing a ministry acceptable to both, is another sign of the times. The amazing thing is, that that joint committee has been able to agree unanimously upon a report, which is now before the churches concerned for their consideration.

All these things, and many more that I could mention if there were time, prove beyond question that some progress has been made, and in some respects at least, Canada is a better and finer place in which to live than it was in 1897. We must not assume, however, that the final goal has been reached. Far, far from it. Great evils still flourish in Canada. They threaten the welfare of our people and are a constant challenge to the Christian church. Two devastating wars have not only slaughtered thousands of our finest youth, but have seriously damaged our moral standards. A materialistic outlook on life, the making of money and the seeking of pleasure have become dominant in the lives of many. At the beginning of this century only nineteen divorces per year were granted in Canada. The number is now over 7,500 per year. The home is the basic institution of human society. That which threatens or undermines the home strikes a vital blow at the welfare of man. The liquor traffic is increasing in power, levying its toll upon human life, and seriously interfering with the welfare of the people. At the same time, its domination of government through its enormous financial power, threatens democracy itself.

Social injustice compels thousands of Canadian families to live on incomes far below the standard of decency and comfort, and condemns many children to grow up in dens unfit for human habitation. According to the census of 1941 thirty per cent. of the families in Toronto had incomes less than the amount declared by the Toronto Welfare Council as a minimum for "health and decency." After family allowances were introduced only about twenty-four per cent. of Toronto families were below the minimum; but of the families with four children forty-two per cent. were below, with five, fifty per cent. below and of those with six children sixty per cent. were below the standard of health and decency—this in a land of plenty and in a time of boasted prosperity. Franklin Roosevelt declared that when he took office, one-third of the American people were inadequately fed, clothed and housed. Canada was little if any better. When the Second War came, thousands of young Canadians were rejected for military service, because of defects due to malnutrition in their growing years.

Racial discrmination and antagonism are rampant. The most striking and at the same time most disgraceful demonstration of that is the recent treatment of our Japanese Canadian fellow-citizens. Many of these people, born in Canada, as loyal to Canadian institutions as any, simply because they were born of Japanese parents, have been herded into concentration camps, their property confiscated and sold at ridiculously low prices. They have been deprived of the right to vote, the right to hold property and the opportunity of carrying on their business when and where they chose. It cannot be denied that the exigencies of war called for some effective action by the government, that would protect the interests of the nation, but now that peace has come, there is no excuse for continuing this policy of discrimination. Until this wrong has been righted, decent, intelligent Canadians will find it difficult to hold up their heads and take pride in Canadian citizenship.

Finally, as we all know, the atomic bomb threatens to wipe out all the glorious achievements of the human race. This power, wisely and properly used, might confer unthought of blessings on humanity, but if used as an instrument of destruction, will bring universal suffering and loss. Representatives of the nations of the world have been holding meetings for over two years, but international jealousy, suspicion, selfishness and racial antagonism have made their efforts up to the present almost futile.

The root of all this trouble in the world is moral and spiritual. Economic and political methods are very important, but if the hearts of men were right and their attitude to each other in harmony with the spirit of Christ, they could find ways of solving economic and political problems. If this is true, then the only hope of salvation for the world lies in the renewal of spiritual life and of moral power in the lives of men. As Christians we believe that the Gospel of Jesus Christ, and that alone, if effectively applied, can save society. This surely constitutes an inescapable challenge to the Christian church. Her responsibility in this tragic hour is simply tremendous. Because I believe this with all my heart and because I also believe in the final triumph of good over evil, I declare here tonight that if by some magic I could be transported back to that Sunday morning in June, 1897, I would again kneel at the altar of this church, take the vows I took then and dedicate my life to Christ and His Kingdom.

In these fifty years I have made many mistakes. Some things I did which I would not do at all, now. Others I would do differently, and I hope, much better. But there are two things I would not change. First, I would choose the same life partner, if she would have me, and (incredible as it is to me) she says she would. Throughout these fifty years she has been my closest companion, my wisest counsellor, and my soundest critic. She maintained a home life of such a character that in it I found the rest and peace, the inspiration I needed for the battles I had to fight. Her faith and courage supported me in many a trying situation.

Secondly, in spite of many disappointments and of much disillusionment, as I have already said, I would, if I had to make the decision again, give myself to the Church and the work of preaching the Everlasting Gospel of Jesus Christ.